RADICAL HOPE

resurrection faith

in a hurting world

chris price

Radical Hope: Resurrection Faith in a Hurting World

Published by: Apologetics Canada Publishing
32040 Downes Road, Abbotsford, BC, V4X 1X5 Canada

ISBN-13: 978-1530130344

Cover design and layout: Lucas Bergen | hello@lucasbergen.ca

"Our lives are full of brokenness and in need of Radical Hope. Chris's fast-paced investigation is a great place to begin." —Andy Steiger, Director of Apologetics Canada & author of *Thinking? Answering Life's Five Biggest Questions*

"Radical Hope is a thoughtful investigation of Christianity's claim that Jesus conquered death. Chris has written in a way that is compelling and readable without compromising an ounce of intellectual credibility. Everyone, from the thoughtful atheist to the sincere Christian, should give this a read." —Jason Ballard, Host of the *Alpha Youth Film Series*

Where is the wise man? Where is the scholar? Where is the philosopher of this age? Has not God made foolish the wisdom of the world? For since in the wisdom of God the world through its wisdom did not know Him, God was pleased through the foolishness of what was preached to save those who believe. Jews demand miraculous signs and Greeks look for wisdom, but we preach Christ crucified: a stumbling block to Jews and foolishness to Gentiles, but to those whom God has called, both Jews and Greeks, Christ the power of God and the wisdom of God. For the foolishness of God is wiser than man's wisdom, and the weakness of God is stronger than man's strength.

– The Apostle Paul (1 Corinthians 1:20-25 NIV)

radical hope

CONTENTS

INTRO

an unlikely tale

I grew up attending church and faith has played an important role in the life of my family for generations. At a young age I frequented a Southern Baptist congregation filled with pews and hymns, but conspicuously empty of young people. In those early years I think I may have smelled the distinct odour of irrelevance that seemed to cling to the institutional church, making it an unlikely refuge for an insecure, coming of age, punk. Plus, I heard the church was filled with hypocrites and, frankly, though I may have been consistently inconsistent, I was proud of the fact that I could forgive myself without the tedious rituals and rigors of conventional religion.

My two younger sisters were different. They whole-heartedly embraced Christianity in their younger years, but even with their marked enthusiasm for all things Jesus, the Christian message just didn't work its way into my heart. I still went to church during this time (I didn't have much choice), but I remember attending services as a teenager hung-over and desperately ill from the previous night's misadventures, even to the point of once having to flee the uncomfortable pew in the middle of a preach to hurl in the bathroom. Little did anybody know that the young man puking in the stall would be the future pastor of the very church he was forced to frequent in his youth. I certainly wouldn't have guessed it.

In my teen years I gladly threw myself into a life-style of drinking heavily, smoking weed, eating magic mushrooms and snorting cocaine on my parents' dresser where they kept their Bible. I lived the party lifestyle and it had its enjoyable moments and its heartbreaking moments, kind of like life in general. Nevertheless, slowly and over time, things began to shift within me. I'm afraid here is where the story might get boringly predicable because I can honestly say that the bottom fell out of the fun. Not to sound overly dramatic, but it felt like I was left staring into a yawning chasm of purposelessness; a void I couldn't fill with sex, drugs or alcohol. I know this all sounds terribly cliché, but in my defense, it doesn't feel cliché when you are living it. At times my life truly felt dark. My hope was fleeting and my happiness was often chemically induced but, try as I might, I couldn't seem to shake my upbringing. I wanted to, sometimes desperately, but those countless tales of sin and grace, judgment and mercy, love, suffering and redemption, all of which never quite worked their way into my heart while I was young, still clung to the 'outside' of my soul like stucco to a wall.

Through a series of events, involving ups and downs too long and arduous to describe here, I was reintroduced to the God of my youth whom I hadn't really known. I trusted in Jesus to save me from my sins and my stubborn self-centered bent and make me new. That was a lot of years ago and following Jesus has made my life harder and weirder, but pursuing Jesus has also made my life better, broader, richer and fuller. God has done remarkable things in my life and in the lives of people I know. I believe I have encountered what the New Testament would call the Spirit of the living Christ.

don't drink the kool-aid

I became a Christian fifteen years ago and looking back I am still struck by the fact that, at the center of the Christian story are some hard-to-stomach beliefs. I grew *out* of Santa Claus, but I grew *into* Christianity. And now, as a thinking adult, I sincerely believe that there is one God in three Persons, Father, Son and Holy Spirit, a belief that requires an odd, paradoxical type of divine arithmetic. I believe that the second member of the Trinity, God the Son, took on humanity in Jesus Christ, making Him the God/man, a clever name for a superhero that Marvel has yet to tap into. I believe that Jesus lived the life we should have lived without sin, and then died the death we should have died for our sins, making Him our divine benefactor paying the debts we alone owe. I believe that three days later Jesus rose bodily[1] from the dead in a transformed, physical body never to die again and that His resurrection is the lynch-pin of the Christian faith, apart from which Christianity is a foolish waste of time and should be abandoned. I believe all this and more. And to think – I used to be so normal!

Can we be honest with each other for a moment and just admit that, at times, the Christian story sounds straight-up crazy and when sane people start to believe crazy things usually religion is involved. I have wrestled with a lot of the objections to Christianity that swirl around beliefs like the Trinity, the doctrine of hell, or the reality of suffering and evil but, to be honest, there is a more fundamental question that must be addressed before an individual explores those other important issues. After all, the belief at the center of the Christian faith is that Jesus rose from the dead, and all of Christianity hinges on this one truth claim. As the apostle Paul wrote, "If Christ has not been raised, your faith is futile; you are still in your sins."[2] For the Christian, a whole lot rides on the resurrection of Jesus and, to be frank, the resurrection itself is not without significant objections that must be addressed in a thoughtful and thorough manner.

"The resurrection of Jesus is just borrowed from pagan mythology. The first Christians were just copycats."

---

1   I will use the phrase 'bodily' throughout the course of this book to make it clear that the resurrection is not just a beautiful metaphor or an interesting way of stating that Jesus went to be with God in heaven after He died.

2   1 Corinthians 15:17 Scripture quotations are taken from the NIV (1984).

"Don't you know that dead people stay dead?"

"The evidence against a resurrection will always be greater than the evidence for a resurrection."

"Science has convincingly shown us that the resurrection is a primitive belief that is no longer sustainable in the face of modern knowledge. You went to college. You should know this. Stop embarrassing yourself."

"Jesus is a historical figure, and by all accounts I am sure he was an interesting guy, but all of those stories about miracles and a resurrection from the dead are later legends that developed over time. Jesus would probably roll *over* in his grave if he heard that people were claiming he arose *out* of his grave."

"How can you believe something so absurd?"

"Do we even know if Jesus actually existed?"

I've heard or read all of the above criticisms and I've felt the weight of *some* of these objections. Truth be told, I don't want to unquestioningly 'drink the cool-aid' either, if you know what I mean. That is why intellectual doubt is not always a bad thing because it can function as an invitation to engage in a deeper exploration of one's faith, to plumb the depths of one's beliefs; for a brief moment, to submerge oneself in the waters of skepticism only to be delighted in the end that your Christian faith is credible enough to keep you afloat, even in the choppy waters of cultural criticism. A stronger faith is often waiting on the other side of tackling your doubts, and that is what I am inviting you to do in this book.

I hope to address head-on the doubts concerning the resurrection, and in response to present you with the clear and compelling historical reasons that have strengthened my belief that Jesus died and three days later God raised Him bodily from the dead.[3] All of which means, among other things, that we can encounter the risen Christ today in the midst of our doubt, in the shifting sands of our skepticism, and in the depths of our pain, fears and longings. He lives to make us new, to heal our hearts and transform our lives.

If the Christian claim is true, the resurrection becomes our radical hope in a hurting world. Death, our great enemy, has been defeated through the dying and rising of the Son of God. But is this hope built on a solid foundation? Are there sound and satisfying reasons to believe that God raised Jesus from the dead? I invite you to turn the page with me and discover the answers to these questions and more.

---

3   For the purpose of clarity, it is also important to note that the orthodox Christian belief is that God raised Jesus from the dead in a transformed *physical* body, a different mode of bodily existence, fully animated by God's Spirit, all of which stretches the descriptive power of our language to its limits. I mention this only so that, as readers, we distinguish Jesus' resurrection from various individuals like Lazarus, who died and were raised from the dead, only to later die again (John 11). Lazarus underwent a revivification. Jesus conquered the grave never to die again and in doing so is the first and best of those who will be resurrected to an eternal life with God at the end of the age (1 Corinthians 15).

CHAPTER ONE

jesus lived and died

Imagine you could move into any neighbourhood your heart desired and money was no object. What area code would you gravitate towards? Would you put down roots in a high-income area with phenomenal schools, state-of-the-art recreational facilities, and neighbours who actually mowed their lawns on a consistent basis? That all sounds fantastic to me.

Unfortunately, many of us find ourselves without the means to pick and choose the various locales we plant our families in and, even if we appreciate our neighbourhood, we are frequently aware that circumstances could be fairer, roads could be less busy, neighbours could be more friendly, dogs could bark at a more reasonable volume, and property taxes could be less onerous.

God is rather lucky in this regard. God, the Creator and Sustainer of heaven and earth, would have no such constraints. If God desired to move into a certain area code He would have unlimited resources at His disposal. When you own everything, prime real estate is not hard to come by.

And, remarkably, the Christian story *is* about God moving into a specific neighbourhood, at a precise moment in time. Yet, when the author of history casts Himself in the leading role in His own drama, the type of town He graced with His presence should come as a shock to us.

The Gospel accounts tell us that in some mysterious way God, in Jesus, moved into an impoverished neighbourhood, a small town barely worthy of putting on the map, into a family with little money and even less respect, constantly shrouded in the rumours of Mary's alleged infidelity. (That whole virgin birth thing was hard to swallow, even back then!) Not only that, but Jesus moved into an occupied nation, crushed under the heels of Roman soldiers, and taxed into oblivion. He, with His family, even experienced refugee status in Egypt for a time. God, in Jesus, chose the cramping restrictions of poverty; He selected for Himself rejection and suffering instead of prestige and wealth. This is the neighbourhood that the one and only Son of God moved into, the type of block we only visit by accident and then only with our car doors securely locked.

It is a miracle of grace that there were no extenuating circumstances that forced God to do this. It wasn't like the mortgage in heaven was just too steep so God had to slum it out on earth. God did this because God wanted to do this. God wanted to be with us, with you. Jesus *is* God with us, our hope in a hurting world. This is a beautiful story, it stirs the soul and I wish it were true. But, is it?

Prior to looking at the evidence for the resurrection, we must examine briefly the historical evidence for the life and death of Jesus. We will spend little time here as very few, if any, serious historians deny that Jesus lived and died. In the same way that you seldom explain the large wake in the water by denying the existence of a boat, you don't explain the enormous wake left by Jesus' life, including the shape that early Christianity took, by denying the existence of Jesus. Nevertheless, I must begin by stating the obvious truth that, in order for Jesus to rise bodily from the dead, He would first have to live and die.

method

Before I dig into the evidence, a few words about my method in the pages that follow might be helpful for the reader. First, I am a pastor who believes that the Bible is God's Word. I want to state that up front. Throughout the course of our journey together, however, I will not assume that the Bible is divinely inspired. Instead, I will put my view of scripture to one side and build my case on the bedrock historical data that emerges from sources both inside and outside of the New Testament. I will quote the scriptures, but this should not confuse the reader into thinking that I am referencing it as an infallible divine revelation, but rather as a historical source.

As a Christian pastor with a high view of scripture this might strike the reader as an odd approach to take, but this concession is for the sake of the vast majority of people who do not and, in some cases, find they cannot believe that the scripture is divinely inspired. The approach popularly summarized as, 'The Bible says it, I believe it, that settles it' may work for the believer, but it gets very little traction with the non-believer who is not even willing to admit the historical accuracy of the Bible, let alone its divine origin. I am attempting to meet the skeptic on their turf and show that, even with this major concession, the historical evidence strongly suggests that God raised Jesus of Nazareth from the dead.

Second, it is also worth mentioning that I will quote a lot of skeptical voices that do not believe in the orthodox Christian faith. The value of using the skeptic, or hostile witness, is that when a point of agreement regarding the reliability of a certain piece of data is acknowledged between two scholars with radically different worldviews, our confidence in the trustworthiness of the information in question should be considerably strengthened.

When it comes to the historical evidence for the life and death of Jesus, both of these brief explanations about method become extremely important to remove any accusation of unfair bias. So, in what follows allow me to call up to the courtroom stand various skeptical voices that testify with certainty first, to the existence of Jesus, and second, to His violent death on a Roman cross.

the evidence for life

Bart D. Erhman is a superstar in the skeptical community,

the equivalent of hockey's Sidney Crosby, as far as respected and informed critics of Christianity go. Yet Erhman claims that, "He (Jesus) certainly existed, as virtually every competent scholar of antiquity, Christian or non-Christian, agrees based on clear and certain evidence."[4] Though Erhman has written consistently against Orthodox Christian beliefs, his willingness to assert so confidently that Jesus existed is significant. But we don't want to simply depend on his authority as a scholar. Instead we should ask, what is this clear and certain evidence that he references?

extra-biblical sources

For starters, ten writers outside of the New Testament mention Jesus. From their writings alone we can discover that the first Christians worshiped Jesus as God, He was crucified, miracles were attributed to Him, James was His brother and a leader in the early church, and His first disciples claimed that He rose from the dead. In other words, non-Christian authors like Tacitus, Josephus, Pliny the Younger, Lucian of Samosota, Mara Bar-Seraphon and the Jewish Talmud[5] confirm the basic story line of the New Testament.[6]

In one of the Jewish historians' (Josephus) less controversial passages, Jesus is indirectly mentioned. He writes that the Jewish high priest Annas, "convened the judges of the Sanhedrin and brought

---

4   Bart D. Ehrman, *Forged: Writing in the Name of God: Why the Bible's Authors are not who we think they are* (New York, NY: HarperCollins Publishers, 2011), 248.

5   The Jewish Talmud is a reference to a collection of Jewish writings that contains the opinions of many Jewish rabbis. Much of the writing post-dates the Christian era, stretching from the first to the fifth century.

6   Paul Barnett, *Is the New Testament Reliable?* (Downers Grove, Ill: Intervarsity Press, 2003), 34.

before them a man named James, the brother of Jesus who was called the Christ, and certain others. He accused them of having transgressed the law and delivered them up to be stoned." (*Antiquities* 20.197-203) Here Jesus is mentioned as one who was called the Messiah by His followers.

The Roman historian Tacitus wrote these words describing how in the 60s CE the Roman Emperor Nero scapegoated the Christians for a fire that he most likely started in the city of Rome. The passage reads as follows:

> Consequently, to get rid of the report, Nero fastened the guilt and inflicted the most exquisite tortures on a class hated for their abominations, called Christians by the general populace. Christus, from whom the name had its origin, suffered the extreme penalty during the reign of Tiberius at the hands of one of our procurators, Pontius Pilate, and a deadly superstition, thus checked for the moment, again broke out not only in Judaea, the first source of the evil, but also in the City (Rome). (*Annals* 15:44.2-5)

In the above quote, a Roman historian who is not at all friendly to Christian beliefs, confirms the existence of Christ and the fact that He died by crucifixion at the hands of Pontius Pilate, as well as possibly referring to the belief in Jesus' resurrection as a 'deadly superstition'.

Not only do we have these unfriendly sources, we also have the New Testament. The New Testament was not originally written as one book, as is presented to us in our modern Bible. Originally it consisted of twenty-seven separate writings that were later collected by the church into one canonized, authoritative book. Canonization involves the process the church underwent in establishing which writings would be considered normative and authoritative in the life of the church. The criteria and process involved in determining which books would be accepted and which books would be rejected was not an arbitrary one by any means, but I don't have time to discuss it here. Instead, I mention the compilation of the New Testament documents to simply point out that in the New Testament we actually have the existence of Jesus referenced in not just one, but multiple, early and independent sources.

I realize that this is all a little tedious and boring but the end result will be worth it, so brew a pot of coffee, appoint a friend to nudge you if you start dozing, and track with me a bit longer. If the evidences listed above weren't already enough, historians also have the writings of post-apostolic church fathers that frequently mention Jesus. The early church leader, Polycarp, lived and wrote letters to churches in the late first and early second century and he was a disciple of the apostle John, a dear friend of Jesus. Clement of Rome lived and wrote at the turn of the first century and the apostle Paul trained him personally.[7] Other second century church fathers mention crossing paths with people who had personally met Jesus, or had even been healed by Jesus, giving us

---

7   Jim Warner Wallace, *Cold-Case Christianity* (Colorado Springs, CO: David C. Cook, 2013), 222.

more trustworthy evidence for His existence.

Dr. Paul Barnett writes that in his studies he discovered, "The historical evidence for Jesus and the origins of Christianity compared favourably with that available for Tiberius, the Roman emperor in whose time Jesus exercised his ministry, or for Alexander the Great or the emperor Nero."[8] If one were to add up all the non-Christian sources that mention Jesus you would find that He is actually referenced *more* times in the historical literature of that period than Tiberius Caesar and, if you add in the Christian sources, "authors mentioning Jesus outnumber those mentioning Tiberius 43 to 10."[9] Point being, no one would ever think of doubting this Caesar's existence, so why would any honest person ever doubt that Jesus of Nazareth ministered in the first century? In the end, whether one believes the Christian story or not, there is certainly no good reason to deny the existence of the man called Jesus of Nazareth.

death

Most people in the developed world start their life in diapers and end their life in diapers with a lot of quick years in between. Then we die, we pass on, we take a dirt nap, we push up daisies, and we provide worms with an all-you-can-eat buffet. Crass, I know, but factually accurate nonetheless. Every one of us is going to die. Period. So, obviously, it is not very remarkable in itself

---

8   Paul Barnett, *Is the New Testament Reliable?* (Downers Grover, Ill: Intervarsity Press, 2003), 20.

9   Norman Geisler & Frank Turek, *I Don't have Enough Faith to be an Atheist* (Wheaton, Illinois: Crossway Books, 2004), 221.

that Jesus would die. But, before we can effectively investigate the evidence for Jesus' bodily resurrection, we must first be certain that the Romans successfully killed Him when they crucified Him on the cross.

In truth, no credible historian believes that Jesus didn't die on a Roman cross by crucifixion. Once again, let me call to the stand a few skeptical voices. The scholar, John Dominic Crossan, claims, "That [Jesus] was crucified is as sure as anything historical can ever be."[10] Gerd Lüdemann, a New Testament Scholar and himself an atheist, writes, "The fact of the death of Jesus as a consequence of crucifixion is indisputable, despite hypotheses of a pseudo-death or a deception which are sometimes put forward. It need not be discussed further here."[11]

Jesus' crucifixion is mentioned in all four gospels, including the various canonical epistles (letters written to churches by the first followers of Jesus). Jesus' death is also recorded by non-Christian historians like Tacitus (as seen above), Josephus, and the Jewish Talmud and, therefore, is witnessed to in early historical sources with multiple lines of evidence, including skeptical and hostile sources (Tacitus and the Talmud, in particular).

We also know too much about how brutal crucifixion was in the first century to seriously entertain the idea that Jesus' didn't die on a cross. Roman soldiers were professional execu-

---

10   John Dominic Crossan, *Jesus: A Revolutionary Biography* (San Francisco: HarperCollins, 1991), 145.

11   Gerd Lüdemann, *The Resurrection of Jesus Christ: A Historical Inquiry* (Amherst, NY: Prometheus, 2004), 50.

tioners and if a Roman soldier failed in his duty his own life would be forfeited, so they were highly motivated to accomplish the job. To quote a pastor and theologian:

> Jesus was crucified, and a professional executioner declared Him dead. To ensure Jesus was dead, a spear was thrust through His side and a mixture of blood and water poured out of His side because the spear burst His heart sac. Jesus' dead body was wrapped in upwards of one hundred pounds of linens and spices, which, even if He were able to somehow survive the beatings, floggings, crucifixion, and a pierced heart, would have killed Him by asphyxiation. Even if through all of this Jesus somehow survived (which would itself be a miracle), He could not have endured three days without food, water, or medical attention in a cold tomb carved out of rock. In summary, Jesus died.[12]

Jesus clearly could not have survived the cross. Some other religious traditions have suggested that God would not allow a prophet of His to endure such a humiliating death and, therefore, did not allow Jesus to undergo crucifixion but, instead, had a lookalike crucified in His place. This proposal isn't very compelling for a number of reasons. First, this idea originates in a

---

12   Mark Driscoll & Gerry Breshears, *Doctrine* (Wheaton, Ill: Crossway Publishing, 2010), 287.

source[13] that post-dates Jesus' death by around 600 years and it would seem absurd to trust a document written hundreds of years after the events in question over and above the Gospels, which were produce by individuals who, at the very least, were in touch with the actual disciples who were there![14] Second, it displays a surprising lack of awareness about the violent fate that many of God's prophets in the Old Testament endured. Third, it is also theologically troubling to assert that God disguised someone to look like Jesus and had that individual crucified in Christ's place because, to do so, accuses God of radical deception, impugning the trustworthiness of His character. In fact, believing that God played the role of the con artist on the cross means that you can't believe anything else He's ever said; He's already proven to be a deceiver. A God who would willingly deceive like this is ultimately unknowable because any divine revelation from this God could not be trusted.

conclusion

For reasons like those stated above, it should be clear that Jesus not only lived, but also died on a cross. His brutal death was originally a tragedy for His first followers, shattering their hopes and leaving them demoralized, frightened and despairing. That

---

13   The source is, of course, the Koran which reads, "They killed him not, nor crucified him, but so it was made to appear to them, and those who differ therein are full of doubts, with not knowledge, but only conjecture to follow, for a surety they killed him not: Nay, Allah raised him up unto Himself; and Allah is Exalted in Power, Wise." (Sura 4:157-158)

14   Norman Geisler & Frank Turek, *I Don't have Enough Faith to be an Atheist* (Wheaton, Ill: Crossway books, 2004), 309.

is, until something altogether surprising took place; an event so shocking and altogether powerful that it would lead one author, centuries later, to write these moving words about the global influence of Jesus:[15]

> Here is a man who was born in an obscure village, the child of a peasant woman. He grew up in another village. He worked in a carpenter shop until He was thirty. Then for three years He was an itinerant preacher.
>
> He never owned a home. He never wrote a book. He never held an office. He never had a family. He never went to college. He never put His foot inside a big city. He never traveled two hundred miles from the place He was born. He never did one of the things that usually accompany greatness. He had no credentials but Himself...
>
> While still a young man, the tide of popular opinion turned against Him. His friends ran away. One of them denied Him. He was turned over to His enemies. He went through the mockery of a trial. He was nailed upon a cross between two thieves. While He was dying His executioners gambled for the only piece of property He had on earth – His coat. When He was dead, He was laid in a borrowed grave through the pity of a friend.

---

15   Dr. James Allan Francis wrote this in 1926.

Nineteen long centuries have come and gone, and today He is a centerpiece of the human race and leader of the column of progress.

I am far within the mark when I say that all the armies that ever marched, all the navies that were ever built; all the parliaments that ever sat and all the kings that ever reigned, put together, have not affected the life of man upon this earth as powerfully as has that one solitary life.

How did this one short life that ended by crucifixion utterly transform the course of world history? How did Jesus become the most famous, most influential person who has ever lived? The shocking answer is waiting for us.

jesus live and died

CHAPTER TWO
the empty tomb

Have you ever lost something that was precious to you, or thought you had misplaced it only to be overcome with relief when you rediscovered your missing possession? I still remember that afternoon when I left my brand new computer at a local Chinese restaurant only to realize my mistake once arriving back at the office. I sped all the way back to that fine establishment, holding my breath, hoping beyond hope that my computer was where I had left it. You can imagine my gladness when I found my laptop, safe and sound, waiting patiently for me to reclaim it.

I have young children, too, and they never stay in one place. My son once ran away from me while I was paying for groceries, disappearing like a well-trained ninja. One moment he was there and the next moment he had vanished. I couldn't locate him right away so I panicked. The workers, seeing the immediate fear in my eyes, called out a special code over the intercom causing employees to rush to the front doors, barricading the exits. A frantic search began and, thankfully, we ended up finding him in two minutes, but I learned that it is frightfully easy to lose a child in a grocery store.

On the other hand, I imagine that it is extremely difficult to lose a dead body for the simple reason that dead bodies don't move. Zombie apocalypses aside, corpses are very predictable. Lifeless bodies always lose in games of hide and seek. This is obviously true today and it was obviously true two thousand years ago.

In the last section we discussed, albeit briefly, the historical evidence for the life and death of Jesus. Jesus lived, Jesus died and Jesus was buried. The Gospels tell us that He was laid to rest in a tomb. Three days later that same tomb was discovered to be empty. This is where the Easter story starts to get a little more mysterious. Looking at this event from a strictly historical perspective, how can we be reasonably certain that Jesus' tomb was found empty? In what follows, I will provide four lines of evidence, which, isolated from one another may possess varying degrees of persuasiveness, but as an accumulative case strongly suggest the authenticity of the empty tomb story.

the women & the cowardly men

When you read the Gospels, you find that the women were the first to discover the empty tomb (Matthew 28:5-8, Luke 24:1-8).

Why should this simple fact suggest the authenticity of the empty tomb narratives recorded in the Gospels? To answer this question we must understand a bit of the cultural situation pertaining to women. In first century Judaism, women were not allowed to be legal witnesses. Sadly and shamefully, their testimony was not considered valid or taken seriously. There is evidence for this negative view directed towards women in many of the Jewish writings from this era.

> But let not the testimony of women be admitted, on account of the levity and boldness of their sex, nor let servants be admitted to give testimony on account of the ignobility of their soul; since it is probable that they may not speak truth, either out of hope of gain, or fear of punishment. — Josephus

> Any evidence which a woman [gives] is not valid (to offer), also they are not valid to offer. This is equivalent to saying that one who is Rabbinically accounted a robber is qualified to give the same evidence as a woman. — Talmud (Rosh Hashannah)

> Sooner let the words of the Law be burnt than delivered to women. —Talmud (Sotah)[16]

---

16   Quotes culled from this article: http://www.thegospelcoalition.org/article/4-reasons-to-believe-in-the-empty-tomb

The above quotations obviously don't represent a very positive view of women. In light of this cultural context, and the widespread influence of patriarchy, if you are going to fabricate a story about an empty tomb you don't initially make women the first eyewitnesses. That type of literary creation would be a counterproductive detail from an evangelistic and credibility standpoint. Instead it is likely that the women eyewitnesses are included by the Gospel writers simply because they were committed to accurate reportage and it must have been well known that this is, indeed, what had happened.

In addition to this point, in the stories surrounding the crucifixion and resurrection you are presented with the leader of the disciples (Peter) denying Jesus, and many of the other disciples running away discouraged and hiding fearfully behind closed doors when Jesus is killed. In other words, the leaders of the church look like cowards. As an author trying to commend to your audience the legitimacy of your new religious movement, you don't include these embarrassing details about your leaders unless you are remarkably committed to authenticity and telling the truth about what happened, warts and all. Historians would call this the *embarrassment criterion,* which is used to evaluate the reliability of a historical source. Simply stated, when a writer records information that is potentially embarrassing to his or her own interests it is likely that the information is credible and accurate, rather than the imaginative creation of the author for polemical purposes. Both the depiction of the women as witnesses and the cowardly behavior of the disciples, suggest an author interested in accurate reporting, regardless of the embarrassing or ugly light it sheds on the founders of the church.

proximity to jerusalem

The disciples started preaching about the death and resurrection of Jesus in Jerusalem, the very place where Jesus was publicly killed and crucified a few weeks earlier (Acts 2). Amazingly, many believed this message, which would be impossible to imagine if Jesus' body was rotting in the well-known location of a tomb. At the very least, preaching the resurrection in Jerusalem required an empty tomb, otherwise the opponents of Jesus' first followers, which were many in Jerusalem (Acts 4), could have just found the tomb and produced the body. In a hot arid climate such as the Holy Land, even weeks later a partially decomposed body may be recognizable. In fact, even a skeleton would have done the job if produced from Joseph's tomb that was known to be empty before the death of Jesus!

Consider as well that the resurrection of Jesus was the center of the early church's preaching. This dramatic event is mentioned in twelve of the twenty-eight chapters in the book of Acts,[17] which reports summaries of the preaching taking place in the early churches' evangelistic endeavors. For example:

> Fellow Israelites, I can tell you confidently that the patriarch David died and was buried, and his tomb is here to this day. But he was a prophet and knew that

---

17   Mark Driscoll & Gerry Breshears, Doctrine: What Christians Should Believe (Wheaton, Ill: Crossway Publishing, 2010), 295.

God had promised him on oath that he would place one of his descendants on his throne. Seeing what was to come, he spoke of the resurrection of the Messiah, that He was not abandoned to the realm of the dead, nor did His body see decay. **God has raised this Jesus to life, and we are all witnesses of it.** (Acts 2:29-32)

You handed Him over to be killed, and you disowned Him before Pilate, though he had decided to let Him go. You disowned the Holy and Righteous One and asked that a murderer be released to you. You killed the author of life, **but God raised Him from the dead. We are witnesses of this.** (Acts 3:13-16)

We are witnesses of everything He did in the country of the Jews and in Jerusalem. They killed Him by hanging Him on a cross, **but God raised Him from the dead on the third day and caused Him to be seen.** (Acts 10:39, 40)

Therefore since we are God's offspring, we should not think that the divine being is like gold or silver or stone—an image made by human design and skill. In the past God overlooked such ignorance, but now He commands all people everywhere to repent. For He has set a day when He will judge the world with justice by the man He has appointed. **He has given proof of this to everyone by raising Him from the dead.** (Acts 17:29-32)

The first Christians were like a band with one hit song that they played over and over again. In all their preaching they zeroed in on the fact that Jesus died for sins and God raised Him from the dead, giving proof of Jesus' claims and their own that He was and is Messiah, Saviour and Lord. Yet what we *never* read in the book of Acts is a defense of the empty tomb, which, again, makes sense if it was widely known to be devoid of Jesus' body as, indeed, the concept of a bodily resurrection would have already implied to the original Jewish hearers of this message.

joseph's tomb

Joseph of Arimathea was a wealthy man, a member of the Jewish ruling council, and a secret follower of Jesus. When Jesus was crucified Joseph approached Pilate, the Roman governor of the region, and asked for the body with the intention of providing the tomb that was found empty on Easter Sunday.

Not only is Joseph mentioned by all four Gospels, giving us multiple independent records of his involvement in the burial, the figure of Joseph is also not a likely creation of the early church. After all, Joseph was a rich member of the Jewish ruling council in Jerusalem called the Sanhedrin. This was the same council that handed Jesus over to Pilate to be killed and the same council that opposed the preaching of the disciples after the resurrection. As a result there was some understandable resentment between the early Christians and the Sanhedrin, which makes it extremely unlikely that the early Christians would create a story that paints a member of the Sanhedrin in such a great light while, again, simultaneously painting their own leaders as cowards hiding from the authorities in the aftermath of Jesus' crucifixion.

Joseph, it is important to remember, was a prominent, well-known man, so his tomb would have been extremely easy to locate by people in Jerusalem, making it impossible that the disciples, women, or enemies for that matter, could have repeatedly gone to the wrong tomb by mistake. In fact, the tomb, as described in the Gospels, is that of a rich man and these types of burial sites were not exceedingly numerous in Jerusalem, again making it simple to find the tomb and look into the strange events and odd claims made by the disciples.

tomb raiders

Our last piece of evidence is found in the Gospels where it is recorded that the religious leaders, who didn't believe in Jesus' resurrection, offered an early explanation for the empty tomb. They claimed that Jesus' own disciples stole the body.[18] This proposed explanation accuses the disciples of launching a conspiracy and perpetrating a hoax, a significant accusation we will examine later in this book. For now I simply note that this attempted explanation does, in fact, assume an empty tomb as a generally acknowledged fact in Jerusalem.

conclusion

As a result of these four pieces of evidence (and others not mentioned), we are on solid historical grounds when we conclude that the tomb was surely found empty. To be clear, a first

---

18   Matthew 28:13

century death by crucifixion and an empty tomb, by themselves, are not very remarkable and don't require a miraculous explanation. As such, the skeptic shouldn't be too fiercely resistant to the above conclusions. The evidence we explore next, however, puts the empty tomb in an entirely new light.

CHAPTER THREE

the appearances of jesus

I once paid a pastoral visit to a woman who was convinced that her house was haunted. She seemed reasonable, educated, intelligent and fairly skeptical. Her alleged haunting was certainly not a result of wish fulfillment because she found the various 'supernatural' occurrences to be deeply distressing, causing her to contemplate uprooting her family from an otherwise nice home and neighbourhood.

The eeriest part of the story that she shared with me occurred in a bathroom. Her family was outside in the driveway, her husband busily putting the small children into their car seats. She had gone back inside to use the bathroom and, since everyone else was outside, she relieved herself with the door open. The downstairs bathroom was adjacent to the playroom where some of the alleged paranormal activity was centered and, as she sat on her porcelain throne, a small bead flew into the room, struck her in the arm, and bounced into the tub. No one was in the other room. She freaked out, sprinted outside, and hurriedly informed her husband about what had happened. They both immediately searched the house finding no one.

Creepy, I know. I'm still not sure what I think about that whole experience. I believe in a supernatural realm, but I don't know if I believe in ghosts, to be honest. I do know my job can get weird.

Ghosts, visitations, paranormal activity, even zombies, are all the rage in our culture. Many spiritual people claim to have spiritual experiences that involve visions and out-of-body experiences. Could something like an extrasensory, paranormal, or visionary type experience explain what happened to the first disciples after they discovered Jesus' tomb to be empty, which, in turn, led to their belief in the resurrection?

In this chapter we will explore the evidence for the resurrection appearances of Jesus. To begin our investigation we will turn to a letter that the Apostle Paul wrote to the Christians in the city of Corinth.

the church in corinth

Paul wrote the letter we have come to know as first Corinthians sometime in the 50s CE. He penned this letter to a church mired in controversy over a wide range of issues, including skepticism amongst some of the congregants over belief in the bodily resurrection of Jesus. In 1 Corinthians 15 the apostle Paul passes on to this group of believers an early Christian creed that references the resurrection appearances of Jesus to address their skepticism.

The apostle Paul picked up this creed, which is simply a formal statement of belief, while visiting Peter (the leader of the disciples) and James (Jesus' brother) in Jerusalem. Scholars are confident that this short text is a creed that Paul, himself, did not produce based on his use of the traditional rabbinic formula for passing on received tradition: 'what I received I passed on to you.' (1 Cor 11:23; 15:3) In addition, the non-Pauline phrases found in this creed, the use of the original Aramaic name for Peter (Cephas) and the formulaic manner of the writing show that Paul didn't originate this material; rather, he is handing it along to the Corinthians.

The above information becomes incredibly significant to our topic once we realize that historians across the board first, believe this creed to be genuine and, second, date it to within two to five years of Jesus' crucifixion. Some even date it to several months after Jesus' crucifixion! John Dominic Crossan, not by any means a conservative scholar, writes:

> Paul wrote to the Corinthians from Ephesus in the early 50s CE. But he says in 1 Corinthians 15:3 that 'I handed on to you as of first importance which I in turn received.' The most likely source and time for his reception of that tradition would have been Jerusalem in the early 30s when, according to Galatians 1:18,

he 'went up to Jerusalem to visit Cephas [Peter] and stayed with him fifteen days.[19]

According to Crossan (and many others), Paul likely received this information in the early thirties, which means it was written down and passed around prior to that, in the end landing us at a date of composition breathtakingly close to the actual events it records.[20] To have an ancient historical writing, produced by eyewitnesses, so near in time to the events it reports, is source material that historians are prone to drool over.

1 corinthians 15

With the relevant background in mind, let me share with you what 1 Corinthians 15:3-8 actually states:

> For what I received I passed on to you as of first importance: that Christ died for our sins according to the scriptures, that He was buried, that He was raised on the third day according to the scriptures, and that He appeared to Cephas, and then to the Twelve. After that, He appeared to more than five hundred of the brothers

---

19   New York: NY, HarperSanFrancisco, A Division of HarperCollins Publishers, 2001), 254.

20   E.P. Sanders also says: "Paul's letters were written earlier than the gospels, and so his reference to the Twelve is the earliest evidence. It comes in a passage that he repeats as 'tradition', and is thus to be traced back to the earliest days of the movement. In 1 Corinthians 15 he gives the list of resurrection appearances that had been handed down to him." Sanders, E.P., *The Historical Figure of Jesus* (New York: Penguin Books), 1993.

> and sisters at the same time, most of whom are still liv-
> ing, though some have fallen asleep. Then He appeared
> to James, then to all the apostles, and last of all He
> appeared to me also, as to one abnormally born.

Before investigating this creed line by line, I want to re-
mind the reader that, as mentioned earlier, though I believe
the Bible is God's inspired word, I am not quoting it here as
a divine revelation. Rather, I am referencing this text as a historical source, produced by eyewitnesses, dating remarkably
close to the events in question. And, in this early witness to
Christian beliefs, we have recorded for us several resurrection
appearances of Jesus. Let's examine them one by one.

the twelve disciples

First on the list of appearances are the original disciples of Jesus. When Jesus died the disciples were discouraged and fearful.
But, as we saw in the chapter on the empty tomb, a few weeks
later they reemerge as individuals committed to boldly proclaiming the resurrection of Jesus, in many cases to the point of death.
Tradition tells us that Andrew was crucified in Patras, Greece;
Matthew was killed by sword in Ethiopia; Peter was crucified
upside down in Rome; Philip was crucified in Phrygia; Thomas
was stabbed with a spear in India; and John died in exile on the
Island of Patmos.[21] From disillusioned doubters to martyrs is a

---

21   Jim Warner Wallace, *Cold-Case Christianity: A Homicide Detective Investigates The Claims of the Gospels* (Colorado Springs, CO: David C. Cook, 2013), 115.

remarkable transformation that must be explained. What caused this radical shift in belief and behaviour? This early creed tells us that the first followers of Jesus encountered the risen Christ.

the five hundred

Jesus appeared to five hundred individuals at one time, and this testimony becomes even more significant because Paul boldly proclaims that many are still alive, which is an invitation to the Corinthians to check up on his story. You don't give people that type of opportunity if you are fabricating a myth or a lie! Maybe it is just me, but when I lied to my mother during high school, I didn't invite her to investigate the validity of my claims. If I told her that my friend's parents were home when they weren't, I didn't extend her an invitation to visit and snoop around. That would have been counterproductive. The same would be true in Paul's case. Obviously it is a long trip from Corinth to Jerusalem, but Paul made the journey multiple times and it could have been undertaken fairly easily given the relative safety of travel and quality of road ways in the Roman Empire.

This type of authenticity appears to have been a staple of Paul's preaching whenever he undertook the task of testifying publicly about the resurrection of Jesus. He didn't speak solely about an esoteric spiritual experience, but instead, like the other disciples, he pointed to publicly acknowledged events that were open to skeptical inquiry.

One more example of this tendency should be sufficient to support the above point. When Paul found himself on trial before King Agrippa and Festus (Acts 26), he gave a defense for his life and ministry, retelling the dramatic story of his conversion that he also references in 1 Corinthians 15. He ends his testimony by stating to Festus that, "The king (Agrippa) is familiar with these things, and I can speak freely to him. I am convinced that none of this has escaped his notice *because it was not done in a corner.*" The events surrounding Jesus' death and resurrection, and the first Christians' claims about Jesus, were not simply a matter of profound spiritual experiences, accessible only to the individuals undergoing them, but, rather, about public events that could be investigated by anyone interested in a fact-finding mission "because it was not done in a corner".

Again, five hundred people saw Jesus, many are still alive and, in sharing this information, he invites the Corinthians to investigate it for themselves! This willingness to expose his claims to verification should give credibility to Paul's testimony regarding the appearances of Jesus. Paul's inserted comment that some are still living also implies that he may have been personally acquainted with at least a few of these individuals, having interviewed them himself and become convinced of the sincerity and authenticity of their testimony.

james

This early creed also mentions James. The James in question is almost certainly Jesus' brother. Remarkably, James didn't believe in his brother during Jesus' earthly ministry, an embarrassing detail it is unlikely the Gospel writers would have made up. In fact, John 7:5 just states, "For even His own brothers didn't believe in Him." In Mark 3:21, another Gospel writer records that when His family heard about this (His teaching and miracles), they went to take charge of Him, for they said, "He is out of his mind." James doesn't believe in Jesus and, even worse, he thinks that Jesus is out of His mind. The crucifixion would have just confirmed His family's sentiment. Yet we also know, as a matter of history, that James becomes a leader in the early church (Galatians 1, Acts 15), worshiping his brother as Messiah and Lord to the point of eventually dying for that belief.

Josephus, the non-Christian historian, records the context surrounding James' martyrdom in this manner: "When, therefore, Ananus [the High priest] was of this angry disposition, he thought he had now a proper opportunity to exercise his authority. Festus was now dead, and Albinus was but upon the road. So he assembled the Sanhedrin of judges, and brought before them the brother of Jesus, who was called the Christ, whose name was James." (Jewish Antiquities 20.9.1) Josephus goes on to say that James was stoned to death for his belief in his brother, the Messiah.

Ask yourself, what would it take for you to worship your brother as God and then die for that belief? Seriously, think about it. Consider how you treated your siblings, or how they mistreated you in turn. My friend, Peter, grew up with a younger sister. One sunny afternoon Peter etched an X in the ground next to a sprawling oak tree. Above the X dangled a suspicious string, swinging lazily in the breeze, begging to be pulled. Attached to this lonely, strangely out of place string, was a decent sized rock, perched somewhat precariously in the foliage above.

Peter beckoned to his sister, kindly inviting her to tug on the string. What precious trust, the type that exists in the heart of every inexperienced younger sister hoping beyond hope to be invited into the big kid games, was utterly shattered in the quick sequence of events that ensued. The string was pulled and the dangerous prank was played. The rock found its mark on the smooth, soft, unsuspecting skin of his previously unscarred sister's forehead. One hospital trip later and all hope Peter had of convincing his sister of any divine-like benevolence on his part vanished forever. This story was re-told at his sister's wedding and I doubt it will ever be forgotten.

This is the way it has been amongst siblings since the infancy of our race. It is telling that the first pair of brothers in human history experienced conflict, the end result being that Cain murdered his brother Abel. This type of dysfunction is experienced universally to greater or lesser degrees, which could be why we have rarely seen siblings sincerely believe in, and publicly profess, their fervent trust in the divinity of their brother or sister. When a much admired public figure dies, who tends to write the exposé, letting out of the closet all the ugly secrets known only to those closest to the individual? Family members! Family members are the least likely to deify their closest of kin. Siblings tend to expose their famous brothers and sisters, not exalt them to god-like status as adults. It is much harder to hide your flaws at home. Yet James became a prominent leader in a religious community in which these types of claims were made about his brother:

> In speaking about the Jewish people, the apostle Paul writes, "From them is traced the human ancestry of **Christ, who is God over all, forever praised.**" (Romans 9:5)

Or,

> "Yet for us there is only one God, the Father, from whom all things came and for whom we live; and there is but one Lord, **Jesus Christ, through whom all things came and through whom we live.**"
> (1 Corinthians 8:6)

James is one of the overseers of a movement in which his brother, whom he likely lived with under the same roof for a time while growing up, is called God over all, forever praised, and the one through whom all things came to be. And let me be clear as to what I mean when I use the language of deifying a sibling. This is not new-age spirituality or eastern religion. I mean by deity what the word must have meant for James. After all, we are talking about Jewish siblings here. Jesus and James were not new-age mystics comfortable with the claim of inherent divinity shared by all of humanity; they were not Greek polytheists, exceedingly happy to add one more deity to the pantheon of existing 'gods'. They were Jewish boys who from a young age had the belief drilled into their heads that there was (and is) only one God and He alone is to be worshiped; anything less than this unswerving commitment to the Creator of all was idolatrous and worthy of swift condemnation.

All the reliable information we have about James shows him to be a sane, wise, politically savvy leader who was respected by many in Jerusalem. Yet, stunningly, James came to worship his brother as Messiah and Lord, and eventually died for that belief.

An extraordinary occurrence like this requires an extraordinary explanation and here we are given one – the resurrected Christ appeared to James.

paul

Last, and most striking on the list perhaps, is that fact that Jesus appeared to Paul. Paul hated Christians and was hell-bent on destroying the church (Acts 8). What transformed him from a persecutor of Christians to a pastor who was willing to endure extraordinary hardship to proclaim the Gospel? Many modern scholars would offer a variety of opinions in response to this question, so whom should we believe?

Imagine with me that you experienced a dramatic life-change and many different individuals, far removed from your situation or story, had an opinion about the cause of your life-transforming encounter. Would you want the opportunity to explain yourself? And would you like your answer to be taken seriously? After all, we are talking about your life! I think the answer to the above questions would be 'yes', so it is only common decency to give Paul that same courtesy.

You could ask him, "Paul, what dramatically changed your life?"

Or, let's say you were feeling a little more incredulous and combative that day and inquired instead:

"Paul, why would you forsake a fast-track to religious stardom, forgo a cushy life as a well-respected Rabbi, trained under a famous Jewish teacher, toting a Roman Citizenship to boot? Why would you give all of that up to follow a crucified, untrained, itinerant rabbi, without the proper credentials, from a shady background?"

Your strident line of questioning could continue along this vein, mixing in a bit of flattery to soften the aggressive nature of your inquiry:

"Paul, you are not crazy, you are brilliant; I've read your letters, I've been impressed by the depth and breadth of your learning, I've heard it said that a mind like yours comes around only once every five hundred years.[22] I can see you've been trained in classical rhetoric and rabbinic reasoning, so why give it all up for a disgraced Galilean, why bear *His* name? Why suffer hardship and persecution for *His* sake? Why, Paul, why?"

Pretend that you had actually asked Paul those questions. In response he would have only one reply for you, an answer that would have originally shocked him as much as it may currently shock you: Jesus Christ rose from the dead and appeared to me. *That* would be his unapologetic answer.

Curiously, I have books on my shelves written by brilliant, learned authors who deny the resurrection ever took place, sometimes implying (or boldly stating) that Paul can't *actually* mean what he seems to have meant. The copyright date for these published works is usually almost two thousand years after the Easter event in question, making me both wonder how these modern authors know what happened, and question why should I take their word over the eyewitnesses who were there? The modern scholar who denies the resurrection gets published. The Apostle Paul who testified to the resurrection was punished. Not to be uncharitable, or to psychoanalyze scholars I don't personally

---

22   I believe it was the Pauline scholar, Gordon Fee, who made this comment.

know, but I can't help wondering who has greater motivation to fudge the facts: the apostle Paul or his modern exegetes?

One last point before moving on, I know that people tend to believe what they want to believe and religious people, in particular, have a tendency to see 'miracles' in events for which a hard-nosed, skeptical inquirer could find plausible non-miraculous explanations. At times we believe what we long to believe. But, in this case, what we will continue to discover is that this type of wish fulfillment as an explanation for the resurrection appearances probably won't account for James' transformation, and certainly will not work for Paul. The reported appearances to Paul and James indicate that Jesus didn't just reveal Himself to friends or followers who might have been predisposed to think high and exalted things about Him. Rather, Christ appeared to a skeptic and unbeliever (James) and a hostile unbeliever (Paul), meaning that Jesus' appearances didn't just convince *already* believers; His appearances *created* believers. As William Lane Craig stated in his debate with John Dominic Crossan on the resurrection, "The faith of the disciples did not lead to the resurrection appearances, but it was the appearances which led to their faith."[23]

minimal facts

Up to this point in our journey we have explored evidence for the life, death, burial and empty tomb of Jesus. We have also examined a very early tradition, taking us right back to Jesus' first

---

23   Paul Copan, ed., *Will the Real Jesus Please Stand Up? A Debate between William Lane Craig and John Dominic Crossan* (Grand Rapids, MI: Baker Publishing, 1998), 65.

followers, which claims that He appeared to them. As mentioned in the second chapter, a lot of people in Canadian culture don't believe that the Bible is the Word of God. So, for the sake of argument, I have proceeded as though the Bible is not inspired by God and without error. Instead I have tried to move forward as if the New Testament is just a historical document that contains some truth and accurate reportage, possibly muddled together with a whole lot of error, editing, myth-making and embellishment. We are now in a position to further investigate whether or not my significant concession impacts the argument I am developing in these pages.

A scholar named Gary Habermas has done the most comprehensive investigation of the resurrection to date. Habermas has collected more than 1,400 scholarly articles on the resurrection written from 1975 to 2003 by people who approach the Bible as a historical text. Some of these authors believe in God, some do not; some are Christians and some are not. After surveying all of the literature he has come up with a list of bedrock facts that the vast majority of historians and scholars, across the ideological spectrum, are confident occurred. This list of bedrock data will help sum up much of what we've learned thus far in this book. Here are what Habermas calls the minimal facts:[24]

---

24   The list of minimal facts below is from the book, Edited by David Bagget, *Did the Resurrection Happen: A Conversation with Gary Habermas and Antony Flew* (Downers Grove, Ill: InterVarsity Press, 2009), 23. See also, Gary Habermas & Michael Licona, *The Case for the Resurrection of Jesus*, (48-60) for five minimal facts, including: Jesus' death by crucifixion, the disciples believed that He rose from the dead and appeared to them, Paul was converted along with Jesus' brother James, and the tomb was found empty.

1. Jesus died by Roman Crucifixion.

2. He was buried, most likely in a private tomb.

3. Soon afterwards the disciples were discouraged, bereaved, and despondent, having lost hope.

4. Jesus' tomb was found empty very soon after His burial.

5. The disciples had experiences that they believed were actual appearances of the risen Jesus.

6. Due to these experiences, the disciples' lives were transformed. They were even willing to die for their belief.

7. The disciples' preaching about the resurrection took place in the city of Jerusalem shortly after Jesus died and was buried.

8. The gospel message centered on the preaching of the death and resurrection of Jesus.

9. James, the brother of Jesus who was originally skeptical about Jesus, was converted and became a leader of the church in Jerusalem.

10. Saul of Tarsus, an enemy of the church, had an experience he believed to be about the risen Christ.

This is the widely agreed upon data about Jesus and the beginning of Christianity that people have to explain historically. Historians, believing and non-believing, come to identify bedrock historical data by asking a series of probing questions about their sources like: Are there copies of the work that date fairly close to the original? Did the author intentionally undertake the task of communicating reliable history? Are there multiple, independent sources to the event in question? Does the author of the work have a bias that would severely hamper their ability to report accurately what occurred? Does the work contain embarrassing details about main characters being described that suggest authenticity and a commitment to report the truth, even if it is inconvenient to an author friendly to the movement being described? Are events confirmed by witnesses hostile to the events that are being reported?[25] All of these investigative questions, and more, historians ask in an attempt to assess the reliability of their sources. When these criteria are applied to the New Testament as a historical source, which we have already done at various places in this book, they fair remarkably well and lead to historians, across the board, affirming the data listed above.

Once you've agreed on the relevant data, you need to construct a hypothesis that best explains it all.[26] The best explanation will most fully explain the observable data, making it more probable than any rival proposals (this is called the criteria of explanatory scope and power), as well as being implied by a greater variety of accepted truths (the criterion of plausibility). Many individ-

---

25   Some of these criteria are similar to those offered by Gregory A. Boyd & Paul Eddy in their book, *Lord or Legend? Wrestling with the Jesus Dilemma* (Eugene, Oregon: WIPF & STOCK, 2007), 78. But the informed reader will recognize these criteria at play in the work of all New Testament scholars and historians. Multiple attestation, early attestation, enemy attestation, the criterion of double dissimilarity, the embarrassment criterion; all of these and more are used (and sometimes abused) to assess the reliability of historical sources.

26   What makes an explanation best will involve criteria like: explanatory power, explanatory scope, degree of ad hoc-ness, plausibility, coherence etc. Michael Licona's book, *The Resurrection of Jesus*, is a good example of running various scholarly proposals through these criteria.

uals, both scholars and your everyday skeptics, have repeatedly attempted to explain these facts without resorting to God's miraculous intervention. The chart[27] below provides us with the most frequently offered suggestions:

1	Jesus died	Jesus rose bodily from the dead	Christianity
2	Jesus died	Jesus didn't rise—apostles deceivers	Conspiracy
3	Jesus died	Jesus didn't rise—apostles myth-makers	Legend
4	Jesus didn't die		Swoon
5	Jesus died	Jesus didn't rise—apostles deceived	Hallucinations

27   This chart is indebted to Peter Kreeft and his book, *A Handbook of Christian Apologetics*, and its chapter on the resurrection.

Philosopher Peter Kreeft, in his article on the resurrection of Jesus, points out that all of the above options are logically possible (even the first one) so they must all be investigated historically. In what follows we will explore the non-miraculous explanations, ultimately arguing that they cannot compete with the resurrection hypothesis in regard to explanatory power and scope and, though the resurrection seems to fly against firmly accepted truths in human experience making it extremely implausible, this objection is not insurmountable and depends greatly on one's philosophical presuppositions that will be exposed and explored in a later chapter.

CHAPTER FOUR

conspiracy theory

In the late 1960s the Americans sent a man to the moon. Even though I wasn't yet born, I know, almost by heart, astronaut Neil Armstrong's famous words, "That's one small step for man, one giant leap for mankind." What I didn't realize is that, apparently, there is some controversy surrounding this quote and evidence has emerged suggesting that what Armstrong really said was, "That's one small step for *a* man, one giant leap for mankind."[28]

---

28   *http://www.ndtv.com/world-news/is-neil-armstrongs-famous-moon-landing-quote-really-a-misquote-524458* (Accessed January 29, 2016).

I'm not deeply concerned with a misquote, but I am fascinated by those who claim that the American lunar landing footage was faked, involving a conspiracy at the highest levels of the American government. I won't titillate the reader by parading before you all the alleged 'evidence' for this conspiracy theory, but some people certainly believe in it. There is something oddly satisfying about claiming to be one of the few people who are in the know, who see through the commonly held false assumptions believed by the rest of the human 'rabble'. This feeling of superiority is part of the appeal of the conspiracy theory.

Closer to the topic of this book, I still remember when *The Da Vinci Code* was published and people were captivated at the thought that Christianity might involve a larger than life, world-changing, cover-up. I found Dan Brown's best-selling novel to be incredibly gripping, a page-turner to be sure. Yet, despite the popularity of *The Da Vinci Code* and the freshness of its presentation, the skeptical suggestion that some type of conspiracy is responsible for the rise of Christianity is an old one. These conspiracy theorists suppose that the disciples stole the body. They perpetrated a hoax. The first Christians were deceivers who made up the appearances of Jesus, leading to the entire world being changed by a lie!

Claims like this are entertaining and controversial, but does a conspiracy theory actually work as an explanation for the data we've explored thus far? Sadly, to the disappointment of conspiracy theorists everywhere, the fact of the matter is that a put-up job of this nature doesn't hold up well under the type of pressure the first followers of Jesus endured because of their beliefs. In what follows we will expose some of the deficiencies that plague the conspiracy theory hypothesis.

conspiracies break down

Chuck Colson started Prison Fellowship, a significant and noteworthy ministry to inmates in penitentiaries scattered across the globe. Colson's personal story is an interesting one. He was a part of President Nixon's administration and he was involved in the Watergate scandal and the attempted cover up, for which he was imprisoned. He became a Christian in prison and later in life he compared Watergate with the beginning of Christianity. He writes:

> Watergate involved a conspiracy to cover up, perpetuated by the closest aides to the President of the United States—the most powerful men in America, who were intensely loyal to their president. But one of them, John Dean, turned state's evidence that is, testified against Nixon, as he put it, 'to save his own skin'—and he did so only two weeks after informing the President about what was really going on—two weeks! The real cover-up, the lie, could only be held together for two weeks, and then everybody else jumped ship in order to save themselves. Now, the fact is that all that those around the President were facing embarrassment, maybe prison. Nobody's life was at stake.
>
> But what about the disciples? Twelve powerless men, peasants really, were facing not just embarrassment or

political disgrace, but beatings, stonings, execution. Every single one of the disciples insisted, to their dying breaths, that they had physically seen Jesus bodily raised from the dead.

Don't you think that one of those apostles would have cracked before being beheaded or stoned? That one of them would have made a deal with the authorities? None did.[29]

This is a long quote, but the insight provided is worth pondering because it outlines for us the first significant problem facing anyone who sincerely proposes that the disciples colluded together to deceive friends, family members and strangers about Jesus.[30]

Simply put, conspiracies break down under the threat of imprisonment or worse, death, but the disciples proclaimed the resurrection until their deaths. They didn't just lose their freedom like Colson; the disciples gave their very lives.

Brave or foolish people may die for things they believe to be true, or for other various noble reasons, but no sane individual dies for something they know to be false. It has been pointed out

---

29   As quoted in Gary R. Habermas & Michael R. Licona, *The Case for the* Resurrection (Grand Rapids, MI: Kregel Publications, 2004) 94.

30   Elsewhere Colson wrote this, "I know the resurrection is a fact, and Watergate proved it to me. How? Because twelve men testified they had seen Jesus raised from the dead, and then they proclaimed that truth for forty years, never once denying it. Every one was beaten, tortured, stoned and put in prison. They would not have endured that if it weren't true. Watergate embroiled twelve of the most powerful men in the world – and they couldn't keep a lie for three weeks. You're telling me twelve apostles could keep a lie for forty years? Absolutely impossible." Charles Colson, "The Paradox of Power," Power to Change, *www.powertochange.ie/changed/index_Leaders*

to me that, in the Second World War, members of the French underground would lie to the Nazis and die defending that lie in order to conceal information from their enemy. They fabricated a story and willingly died for the deception. This historical example seems like an exception to my above claim, but it actually reinforces the point I am making. The collusion of the members involved in the French Underground likely saved countless lives, helping many people escape Nazi death squads, and we have acknowledged already that brave individuals will die for noble causes.

The disciples' situation was entirely different. For the disciples no lives were spared by telling lies about Jesus' resurrection, rather, lives would only be wasted by this tall-tale, including their own lives, spent frivolously propagating falsehoods until they were silenced by death.

Jim Warner Wallace is a cold case detective who appears on Dateline and he is so gifted as a cold-case investigator that around the show they call him the 'evidence whisperer'. Jim makes the above point most powerfully when he writes:

> Many people are willing to die for what they don't know is a lie. **Martyrdom doesn't confirm the truth, especially when the martyrs don't have first-hand access to the claim for which they're dying. But this wasn't the case for the disciples of Jesus.** They were in a unique position: they knew if the claims about Jesus were true. They were present for the life, ministry, death and alleged resurrection of Jesus. If the claims about Jesus were a lie, the disciples would have

known it (in fact they would have been the source of the lie). That's why their commitment to their testimony was (and is) so compelling. Unlike the rest of us, their willingness to die for their claims has tremendous evidential value. In fact, the commitment of the apostles confirms the truth of the resurrection.[31]

Whereas a transformed life can't prove the truth of any religious claim, the disciples' transformed lives were, according to them, the result of encountering the resurrected Christ and they had no reason to make this story up. Therefore, as Wallace points out, the disciples' eyewitness testimony, and the resulting change in their lives, was and is compelling.

motivation & moral character

The above quote leads us to our second critique of the conspiracy theory which involves the motivation of the disciples to fabricate a story of this nature. Frankly, the disciples didn't have a plausible motivation to tell this lie or create this story. They didn't get money, sex or power – the three things that motivate most deception and crime. In fact, to quote cold case detective Jim Warner Wallace once again:

Sex, money and power are the motives for all the crimes detectives investigate. In fact, these three motives are

---

31   http://coldcasechristianity.com/2015/the-commitment-of-the-apostles-confirms-the-truth-of-the-resurrection/ (Accessed January, 16, 2015).

also behind lesser sins as well. Think about the last time you did something you shouldn't have. If you examine the motivation carefully, you'll probably see that it fits broadly into one of these three categories.[32]

The disciples of Jesus, however, were harassed by the authorities and chased from place to place by religious persecution, all with very little financial recompense. In the book of Acts, when Peter confronts a beggar at the gate called Beautiful, he boldly declares to him, "Silver or gold I do not have"[33] and we have no evidence to indicate that this changed throughout the course of his life and ministry.

The Apostle Paul, himself, had to work as a tent maker to financially support his own preaching ministry. Here is how he describes his labours:

> Five times I received from the Jews the forty lashes minus one. Three times I was beaten with rods, once I was stoned, three times I was shipwrecked, I spent a night and a day in the open sea, I have been constantly on the move. I have been in danger from rivers, in danger from bandits, in danger from my own countrymen, in danger from Gentiles; in danger in the city, in danger in the country, in danger at sea; and in danger from false believers. I have laboured

32   Jim Warner Wallace, *Cold-Case Christianity* (Colorado Springs, CO: David C. Cook, 2013), 241.

33   Acts 3:6

and toiled and have often gone without sleep; I have known hunger and thirst and have often gone without food; I have been cold and naked. Besides everything else, I face daily the pressure of my concern for all the churches. Who is weak, and I do not feel weak?[34]

Paul's testimony is not a rags to riches type of tale. In fact, if he had been motivated to *lose* power, *lose* money, and endure suffering, then, and only then, would becoming a Christian leader have made sense! The disciples achieved minimal power by way of some influence over the fledgling Christian community, but certainly not political power, or the ability to impose their will on people. As for sex, well, there were others ways to have guilt free, promiscuous sex in the first century (like stopping by at the local pagan temple on your way home) and, if that were one's goal, becoming a Christian wasn't the road that arrived at that destination.

In addition, the disciples not only lacked the motivation to create this fiction, they also didn't have the moral character of liars. Jesus' disciples, from all the evidence we have, were transformed by the resurrection into selfless men who served and loved the poor, and provided us with some of our greatest moral teaching.

go to hell

The disciples all believed that hell existed and that leading peo-

---

34   2 Corinthians 11:24-29

ple to worship false gods put your soul at peril. Their own rabbi, Jesus, had described the grisly after-math of a life lived in rebellion against God with striking language:

> I tell you that anyone who looks at a woman lustfully has already committed adultery with her in his heart. If your right eye causes you to stumble, gouge it out and throw it away. It is better for you to lose one part of your body than for your whole body to be thrown into hell. And if your right hand causes you to stumble, cut it off and throw it away. It is better for you to lose one part of your body than for your whole body to go into hell.[35]

According to Jesus, adulterers (defined as those who lust in their heart!) were in danger of God's judgment and, according to the disciples' teaching, so were liars.[36] Regardless of our almost visceral reaction to the doctrine of eternal perdition, don't miss the actual point I am making. Jesus and his followers believed in such a place, and eternal torment is strong motivation to tell the truth if you believe in it and they all did! So, why create a story like this, one that not only gets you very little as far as worldly rewards, but also condemns your soul to damnation?

---

35   Matthew 5:27-29

36   Revelation 21:8

what is the point?

Finally, a conspiracy like this would be dumb, foolish, and idiotic. The disciples were thick headed, at times, but they weren't this foolhardy! An early church writer, Eusebius, put this fictitious speech in the mouths of the disciples, exemplifying this point:

> Let us band together to invent all the miracles and resurrection appearances which we never saw and let us carry the shame even to death! Why not die for nothing? Why dislike torture and whipping inflicted for no good reason? Let us go into all the nations and overthrow their institutions and denounce their gods! Even if we don't convince anybody, at least we'll have the satisfaction of drawing down on ourselves the punishment for our own deceit.[37]

The above speech is intentionally ridiculous, clearly showing forth the absurd nature of proposing that the disciples made up this resurrection story. Granted, an actual resurrection might seem unlikely. But so is a conspiracy where seemingly honest people lie, live difficult lives as a result, and then willingly die horrible deaths for a tall tale they knowingly conjured up. In light of the above criticisms, can we at least agree together that, whatever happened, the disciples were sincere and not intentionally perpetuating a conspiracy? The conspiracy theory, for all its intrigue

---

37   As quoted in William Lane Craig, *The Son Rises: The Historical Evidence for the Resurrection of Jesus* (Eugene, Oregon: Wipf and Stock Publishers, 1981), 24.

and mystery, just doesn't make sense of the data we have.[38] So, now for the moment of decision: In your mind are you willing to agree with me and draw an imaginary line through the conspiracy theory option represented on the chart below because it is a dead end that would take a miracle greater than the resurrection to revive it.

1	Jesus died	Jesus rose bodily from the dead	Christianity
2	Jesus died	Jesus didn't rise— apostles deceivers	~~Conspiracy~~
3	Jesus died	Jesus didn't rise— apostles myth-makers	Legend
4	Jesus didn't die		Swoon
5	Jesus died	Jesus didn't rise— apostles deceived	Hallucinations

---

38   Check out this quote from a well-known, but far from orthodox, New Testament scholar, E.P. Sanders: "That Jesus' followers (and later Paul) had resurrection experiences is, in my judgment, a fact. What the reality was that gave rise to the experiences I do not know. **I do not regard deliberate fraud as a worthwhile explanation.** Many of the people in these lists were to spend the rest of their lives proclaiming that they had seen the risen Lord, and several of them would die for their cause. Moreover, a calculated deception should have produced great unanimity. Instead, there seem to have been competitors: 'I saw him first!' 'No! I did.' Paul's tradition that 500 people saw Jesus at the same time has led some people to suggest that Jesus' followers suffered mass hysteria. But mass hysteria does not explain the other traditions… Finally we know that after his death his followers experienced what they described as the 'resurrection': the appearance of a living but transformed person who had actually died. They believed this, they lived it, and they died for it." E.P. Sanders, *The Historical Figure of Jesus*, (New York: NY, Penguin Books, 1983), 279-280.

CHAPTER FIVE

urban legends & half-dead deities

In 1995 the movie, *Braveheart*, became a blockbuster smash with Mel Gibson playing the Scottish hero, William Wallace. William Wallace was a prominent leader in the Scottish Wars of Independence that raged on during the thirteenth century CE. For his heroic feats Wallace has attained iconic status in Scottish folklore as a brave and fierce soldier whose life was brutally cut short at the hands of the English King, Edward the First.

In the hands of Hollywood, however, Wallace's legacy reached almost legendary heights as a wounded lover, suffering innumerable injustices under British Rule, longing for peace, but forced to fight. And, once he takes up arms, there is almost no stopping Wallace in his quest for justice and freedom. His character flaws and weaknesses are ironed out, or made to seem appealing (like his bloodthirsty desire for revenge against his betrayers) and his virtues are exaggerated to create an inspiring god-like visage, attractive to the modern day moviegoer.

The movie, *Braveheart*, is a small example of how legends begin to grow, build, morph, and evolve over time. You start with an admirable historical figure, place his life and legacy in the hands of a creative talent and, lo and behold, a whitewashed personage appears as a projection of all the best that we find in human nature.

In the previous chapter we explored the failure of the conspiracy proposal. Thankfully for the skeptic, a conspiracy theory is not the only hypothesis on the market. There is also the possibility that the stories of Jesus, recorded many years after he lived and died, are riddled through with legendary material. Is there a legitimate distinction between the Jesus of history and the Christ of faith that is as apparent as the distinction between the William Wilberforce of history and the William Wilberforce of Hollywood box office success? There is much that could be written about this suggestion by way of a response, but let me mention a few notable problems with this popular proposal.

not enough time

In grade ten, my class chartered a yacht to ferry us around an inlet close to where I live. At the end of our tour, as we approached the dock, some of my classmates in a moment of inspired and admired stupidity, launched themselves off the top of the boat into the freezing water and swam to shore. They received a stern slap on the wrist from the administration for their reckless actions. Nineteen years have passed since that epic afternoon. If today I wrote that three students had tragically drowned on that trip and began to spread that rumour around different relational networks with the intention of starting a movement to raise funds in their memories, the story would be short-lived. There are too many eyewitnesses alive today who could refute the false version of the events and would care enough to do so.

In a similar manner, when responding to the legendary proposal one could argue that, when the New Testament documents were finished being written, not enough time had passed, historically speaking, for legends to accumulate around the person of Jesus because too many friendly and hostile eyewitnesses were still alive to contradict false versions of the events. Even if one assumes that the Gospels were written down in their final form upwards of fifty years after the death of Jesus, after many of His contemporaries had long since ceased breathing, the Gospels still contain much earlier source material.

For example, Luke, the author of the Gospel that bears his name, claims to have done significant research in writing his Gospel, an investigation that included interviewing eyewitnesses and reading much earlier accounts of Jesus' ministry that are no longer accessible to us.[39] He begins his account of Jesus' ministry with these words:

---

39   We do know that part of Luke's source material was the Gospel of Mark.

> Many have undertaken to draw up an account of the things that have been fulfilled among us, just as they were handed down to us by those who from the first were eyewitnesses and servants of the word. Therefore, since I myself have carefully investigated everything from the beginning, it seemed good also to me to write an orderly account for you, most excellent Theophilus, so that you may know the certainty of the things you have been taught. (Luke 1:1-4)

Luke sounds like a modern, investigative journalist, deeply committed to accurately reporting the events surrounding Jesus' ministry. And at the beginning of his writing he mentions other records and accounts that pre-date his own Gospel. Luke's writing can be reasonably dated to before both the martyrdom of Paul in the mid-60s CE and the Jewish War, which dated from 66 to 70 CE. It is almost certain that Luke would have mentioned, at least in passing, these two incredibly significant events if his Gospel had been written after their occurrences. The fact that he didn't likely pushes the date of his work to the early 60s, only thirty years after the ministry of Jesus. This in turn means that his source material was produced even earlier, when many eyewitnesses were still alive to be interviewed.[40]

---

40   See. F.F. Bruce, *The New Testament Documents: Are they Reliable?* (Downers Grove, Ill: Intervarsity Press, 1943) for an old but still compelling argument for this dating. N.T. Wright, himself a formidable scholar, has stated that there is no good reason to date any of the Gospels after 70 CE. even though, for the sake of argument, he often dates them later in his writings as it is a concession that doesn't impact his historical argument.

In addition to the Gospels, the various canonical epistles were written close in time, historically speaking, to the ministry and death of Jesus. These letters, like 1 Corinthians 15, contain even earlier material that date remarkably near the events recorded, again, when significant eyewitnesses were still alive, witnesses both favourable and hostile to Jesus, who could have contradicted any false stories circulating about Christ.

All the above constitutes powerful evidence which would counter the legendary hypothesis. Philosopher Peter Kreeft, in his article on the resurrection, points out that a nineteenth century scholar, Julius Muller, "challenged his nineteenth-century contemporaries to produce a single example anywhere in history of a great myth or legend arising around a historical figure and being generally believed within thirty years after that figure's death. No one has ever answered him."[41]

wrong genre

When Jesus told His disciples that He was the gate for the sheep,[42] He didn't expect them to reach for a latch concealed under His robes. To correctly understand literature requires, at the very least, a cursory knowledge of different literary genres and the ability to discern whether or not one is speaking literally or metaphorically. Poetry, for example, should not be read in a manner similar to historical narrative. In a similar way, when it comes to critiquing the legendary hypothesis, genre is a key issue. The fact

---

41   Peter Kreeft & Ronald K. Tacelli, *Handbook of Christian Apologetics* (Downers Grove, Ill: InterVarsity press, 1994), 191.

42   John 10:7

of the matter is the New Testament accounts don't contain the literary characteristics of legendary material. C.S. Lewis, a literary historian and a lover of pagan myths, was merciless on hammering home this point. For example, he wrote,

> I have been reading poems, romances, vision-literature, legends, myths all my life. I know what they are like. I know that not one of them is like this. Of this text there are only two possible views. Either this is reportage...Or else, some unknown writer in the second century, without known predecessors or successors, suddenly anticipated the whole technique of modern, novelistic, realistic narrative. If it is untrue, it must be narrative of this kind. The reader who doesn't see this has simply not learned to read.[43]

In Lewis' learned and expert opinion, whatever else the Gospels are, they are certainly not legends. Unless one is assuming that any literature that contains miracles is automatically in the category of legend, which is a philosophical judgment not a literary one, then it is clear that the Gospels are not in the same literary category as Aesop's fables.[44]

To reference the Gospel of Luke and the Book of Acts again, it is worth noting that there are at least 84 historical facts, verified

---

43   C.S. Lewis, "Modern Theology and Biblical Criticism." In, *The Collected Works of C.S. Lewis* (New York, NY: Inspirational Press, 1996), 281.

44   See also Appendix One for a refutation of the proposal that the Gospel writers were ripping off pagan mystery religions to produce material on Jesus.

by archaeology and other ancient records, that Luke got right, including the cultural practices of certain areas, the names and correct designations of various rulers, ancient trade routes and even the depth of water in certain harbours.[45] This stunning accuracy leads one to conclude that, if Luke is so precise in regard to such incidental matters, it seems safe to assume that he was accurate when it came to more significant issues like the teachings and miracles of Jesus. Evidence like this also counters the suggestion that the Gospels are legendary. After all, legends do not attempt to be historically accurate, whereas the Gospel writers, wherever we can check up on them, have proven to be accurate historians again and again.

the conspiracy theory repackaged

At this point, I am more than ready to put the legendary proposal to bed, but I have one more protest to pen. Simply stated, the legend theory is nothing more than the conspiracy theory repackaged. My reason for this suggestion is the testimony of Jesus' own disciples below:

> We did not follow cleverly invented stories when we told you about the power and coming of our Lord Jesus Christ, but we were eyewitnesses of His majesty. (2 Peter 1:16)

---

45   Norman L. Geisler & Frank Turek, *I Don't Have Enough Faith to Be Atheist* (Wheaton, Illinois: Crossway books, 2004), 256-257.

That which was from the beginning, which we have heard, which we have seen with our eyes, which we have looked at and our hands have touched – this we proclaim concerning the Word of life. (1 John 1:1)

Many of the first Christians were adamant in their writings that they were not making up stories, so to accuse them of fabricating myths is to call them liars and we are right back at the conspiracy theory; a theory that we've already concluded doesn't work. So let's cross the legendary hypothesis off the list.

1	Jesus died	Jesus rose bodily from the dead	Christianity
2	Jesus died	Jesus didn't rise—apostles deceivers	~~Conspiracy~~
3	Jesus died	Jesus didn't rise—apostles myth-makers	~~Legend~~
4	Jesus didn't die		Swoon
5	Jesus died	Jesus didn't rise—apostles deceived	Hallucinations

swoon

Before moving on to the next chapter, I have to mention in short fashion that some authors have argued that it is possible that Jesus didn't really die on the cross. Instead, He passed out from pain and exhaustion, was laid in the tomb, only to regain consciousness shortly thereafter, tracking down the disciples and convincing them that He had conquered the grave. This proposal is not worthy of its own chapter and I don't want to spend a lot of time here because we have already responded to it, albeit briefly, earlier in this book. I will reiterate a few of the reasons that were previously listed, as well as adding two new complaints here.

First, the Romans were very accomplished at killing people on the cross. Second, if a Roman soldier failed in his duty to ensure the prisoner was dead his own life would be forfeited. Soldiers were, therefore, highly motivated to finish the job. Third, and most significant in my mind: As if a half-dead Jesus, feeble from exhaustion and the loss of blood, weakly knocking at the door to the disciple's dwelling, only to slump to the ground in utter fatigue and overwhelming pain as the door opens, could have convinced them that He had somehow conquered the grave as the resurrected Lord of life and vanquisher of death! That just doesn't make sense. Lastly, this pseudo-explanation is also just a repackaging of the conspiracy theory because all of the disciples claimed that Jesus died. And, once again, the conspiracy theory is a dismal failure as an explanatory hypothesis for the concrete historical data surrounding the Easter event. Three non-supernatural explanations down, one to go.

1	Jesus died	Jesus rose bodily from the dead	Christianity
2	Jesus died	Jesus didn't rise— apostles deceivers	~~Conspiracy~~
3	Jesus died	Jesus didn't rise— apostles myth-makers	~~Legend~~
4	Jesus didn't die		~~Swoon~~
5	Jesus died	Jesus didn't rise— apostles deceived	Hallucinations

CHAPTER SIX

when hallucinations happen

I have been told that belief in God is an influential, persistent, all-pervasive form of wish fulfillment. My faith in a Heavenly Father figure is the result of my thoughts, desires and longings projected onto an otherwise cold and uncaring universe. Whereas the philosopher Friedrich Nietzsche claimed that 'God is dead', Sigmund Freud was inclined to think that 'God is dad',[46] the image of the dad we all wished we had. It is out of Freud's thought and

---

46   I first heard this line while watching a debate between Douglas Wilson and Christopher Hitchens.

the earlier philosophizing of the radical German thinker, Ludwig Feuerbach, that the concept of religious belief as a specimen of wish fulfillment became prominent. There is no God, but we wish there were (at least some of us do), so we believe in something that isn't real. God, it could be said, is the ultimate hallucination. Some skeptics have applied a similar idea to the concept of the resurrection. The first disciples were devastated by the death of Jesus and, in their grief, they longed for His return. Out of these longings they projected the appearances of Jesus that lead to a belief in the resurrection and the birth of the Christian church.

After all, it *is* very unlikely that the disciples were intentional deceivers. Instead, perhaps it is more charitable to assume that they were simply deceived themselves. The disciples were sincere, to be sure, but they were sincerely wrong about what they thought they experienced. They no doubt fervently believed they had seen real appearances of Jesus, but they really just underwent hallucinations or grief-induced visions. Consider Peter as a case study. Isn't it possible that Peter was so torn up about denying Jesus and His subsequent death that he conjured up a mental projection of Christ that gave him peace, which he then shared with the disciples and they had similar experiences? The disciples had a 'resurrection' of the heart, or a visionary experience like Peter's that they interpreted through the Jewish category of resurrection.

For the sake of this chapter I am going to treat hallucinations and various visionary phenomena as basically equivalent because the main thrust of this explanatory approach is to imply that the disciples witnessed something that was not objectively real or publicly accessible. Hallucinations, in all of their various types, whether auditory, tactile, or visionary, are false perceptions of something that is not truly there.[47] Whereas almost all serious scholars in the last century or so have abandoned the proposals discussed earlier in this book because of their numerous deficiencies (the legendary theory not withstanding), various versions of the hallucination hypothesis still have some traction having been suggested by some able and current scholars like Gerd Lüdemann, Marcus Borg, Geza Vermes, John Dominic Crossan and others. But does a hallucination or some sort of vision work as an explanation of the data discussed through the course of this book? In what follows, I will present eight reasons why the hallucination hypothesis fails to convincingly explain the minimal facts listed earlier in this book.

what about the empty tomb?

Hallucinations or visions don't explain the empty tomb. If the appearances of Jesus were just hallucinations or visionary experiences, His body would still be in the tomb and the enemies of the early Christian movement would have just produced the body. To quote Dr. William Lane Craig, "Jesus' body was not to be found. That is the decisive argument against the religious hallucination hypothesis. For it is impossible that Jesus' followers could have believed that He was raised from the dead if the corpse were there before them in the tomb."[48] With a definite statement like

---

47   Gary R. Habermas & Michael R. Licona, The Case for the Resurrection of Jesus (Grand Rapids, MI: Kregel Publications, 2004), 105.

48   William Lane Craig, The Son Rises: The Historical Evidence for the Resurrection of Jesus (Eugene, Oregon: Wipf and Stock Publishers, 1981), 35.

Dr. Craig's I could almost stop right there, but I have seven more noteworthy criticisms of this theory to communicate below.

the things navy seals see

Hallucinations rarely, if ever, drastically transform an individual's life. Navy Seals, during a period of training referred to as 'hell week', experience conditions of hunger and exhaustion that are conducive for hallucinations to occur. As a result, some researchers have studied the nature of hallucinations by investigating the experiences of Navy Seals during this intensive stretch of training. For example, in one instance the soldiers were out on the water and an individual was so convinced that he saw a train headed straight for the boat that he jumped into the water, abandoning ship! Other interesting hallucinations, like a waving octopus, were also reported. Yet in each instance the soldiers were talked out of the reality of their hallucination by two common factors: first, those types of things don't happen and, second, their fellow soldiers did not see what they saw. The result was that no lasting life transformation or altering of prior beliefs occurred after the hallucination event.[49] This is, of course, exactly what did *not* happen with the disciples![50]

hallucinations fly solo

Clinical psychologist, Dr. Gary Collins writes, "Hallucina-

---

49   Gary R. Habermas & Michael R. Licona, *The Case for the Resurrection of Jesus* (*Grand Rapids, MI: Kregel Publications, 2004*),106.

50   See. Edited by David Bagget, *Did the Resurrection Happen? A Conversation with Gary Habermas and Antony Flew* (Downers Grove, Ill: InterVarsity Press, 2009), 41.

tions are individual occurrences. By their very nature only one person can see a given hallucination at a time. They certainly are not something which can be seen by a group of people...Since a hallucination exists only in the subjective, personal sense, it is obvious that others cannot witness it."[51] Therefore, a hallucination doesn't explain the appearances of Jesus to groups of people. Just as we saw with the soldiers, and as corroborated by the expert witness, hallucinations are not group events; they are individual occurrences. People don't share hallucinations just like people don't share dreams.[52]

In fact, in the relevant literature, do you know which segment of the population is most likely to experience hallucinations? The answer is not teenagers on acid or mushrooms, though that example would work for this illustration. The group of people most likely to have a hallucination is senior adults bereaving the loss of a loved one. In 39 percent of the cases the seniors studied sensed the presence of their loved one in the room. Only seven percent have a visual perception of their loved one. This means that in the group most vulnerable to visionary hallucinations only seven percent actually have a visual perception of their loved one, so it is both very rare *and* it is never shared. To conclude this objection, we know of no group hallucination ever occurring on record, therefore, it is extremely unlikely that one could account for the appearances of Jesus to groups of individuals, such as the twelve disciples or the

---

51   Josh McDowell & Dave Sterrett, *Did the Resurrection Happen...Really?* (Chicago, Ill: Moody Publishers, 2011),125.

52   Gary R. Habermas & Michael R. Licona, *The Case for the Resurrection of Jesus* (*Grand Rapids, MI: Kregel Publications, 2004*), 106.

500 people mentioned by Paul in 1 Corinthians 15.[53]

james & paul

A hallucination resulting from grief doesn't explain the appearance to the apostle Paul who was not predisposed to have a grief-induced vision or some other type of subjective projection of Jesus. The same would likely be true for James, the brother of Christ. To quote Dr. Gary Habermas, an expert in these matters:

> Although we do not have as much information about James and his frame of mind after Jesus' death as we do for Paul, there is no indication that James was stricken by grief over his brothers' death. As discussed earlier, during Jesus' life, James did not believe that his brother was the Messiah. In fact, it seemed that he was among those who thought that Jesus was deluded. It is unlikely that a pious Jewish unbeliever – who would have viewed his crucified brother as a false messiah who had been cursed by God – was in the frame of mind to experience a life-changing hallucination of the risen Jesus, a hallucination so powerful that it would motivate him to alter his religious beliefs in an area that he believed would cost him his eternal soul if he was mistaken.[54]

---

53   See again the writings of Michael R. Licona and Gary R. Habermas.

54   Gary Habermas & Michael Licona, *The Case for the Resurrection of Jesus* (Grand Rapids, MI: Kregel Publications, 2004), 107-108.

In fact, building on the above two criticisms, Jesus' appearances happened to all different types of people, with different psychological make-ups, in all different places, at all different times of the day. The diverse circumstances and environments in which people encountered the risen Christ count strongly against the hallucination hypothesis. Though this could be a stand-alone objection, it may also be worth mentioning in passing that hallucinations are mental projections resulting from pre-existing beliefs and the first disciples, like all first century Jews, had no pre-existing belief that the Messiah would die, rise from the dead and receive a transformed resurrection body in the middle of history.

hungry hallucinations don't happen

The disciples touched Jesus and ate with Him. It should be obvious to the reader that hallucinations don't eat fish at the dinner table in front of a group of people. For example, in Luke's Gospel, the basic reliability of which has already been established earlier in this book (at least in part), he records this appearance of Jesus:

> While they were still talking about this, Jesus Himself stood among them and said to them, "Peace be with you."
> They were startled and frightened, thinking they saw a ghost. He said to them, "Why are you troubled, and why do doubts rise in your minds? Look at my hands and my feet. It is I myself! Touch me and see; a ghost does not have flesh and bones, as you see I have."

When He had said this, He showed them His hands and feet. And while they still did not believe it because of joy and amazement, He asked them, "Do you have anything here to eat?" They gave Him a piece of broiled fish, and He took it and ate it in their presence. (Luke 24:26-43)

Though these types of stories assume the basic reliability of the Gospel narratives, the idea here is that the Gospel writers did not record the appearances of Jesus as a vision or a hallucination, which means that, if this is what truly happened, the Gospel writers were deliberately deceiving their readers.[55] And to accuse the Gospel writers of intentionally misrepresenting what occurred lands us right back at the conspiracy theory, which already stands debunked.

a failure to communicate

The visionary or hallucinatory theory doesn't explain why the disciples used the language of resurrection to explain the proposed visionary encounters with Jesus. This is significant because the word resurrection in first century Judaism meant a transformed physical body at the end of history, a re-embodiment after death. First century Jews, and later Christians, had language

---

55   Along this line of thought, in 1 Corinthians 15 the Greek word translated as 'appeared' is *ophthe*, which refers more naturally to an objective reality seen by the disciples, rather than a subjective experience only accessible by an individual. The Greek word *horama* is more likely to be used in the case of a subjective vision. The writers clearly told the story in a way that indicated Jesus had a transformed physical body that could be touched. A hallucination or vision is a subjective experience with no objective reality.

to describe a visionary experience, but the first disciples didn't use visionary language when they spoke about Jesus' resurrection. All of the stories we have, including our earliest source material, find authors and eye-witnesses going out of their way to suggest that Jesus had some type of trans-temporal, weirdly unique, but altogether physical body that could walk through walls, but also be touched and eat fish. This is an odd manner of trying to communicate that Jesus had only appeared as some-type of visionary apparition.

This is why, lastly, and building on the above point, the New Testament literature is actually careful to distinguish between the resurrection appearances of Jesus, which were of a bodily and physical nature, to later visions of Jesus. For example, compare Paul's encounter with Jesus, which was clearly objective because his traveling companions witnessed something occurring (a light and a voice), with the vision of Jesus that Stephen had while he was being stoned, which was only noticeable to him.[56] Again, the resurrection appearance is clearly distinguished from the later vision of Jesus by all the New Testament writers. This indicates that they knew about visions, but that they chose not to use that language when describing what happened on Easter Sunday.

This is the final critique of the eight and, when considering all of my objections raised in this chapter, I know it can feel a bit overwhelming, almost like drinking from a fire-hydrant. But I wanted to be thorough in the hope of convincing you that this explanation, though still popular in some circles, is extremely

---

56   See Acts 7:54-60, 9:4-9

inadequate, leaving us with the only proposed theory that the church has ever offered. The disciples were not deceived or deceivers and they were not foolish myth-weavers. Instead, Jesus died was buried and three days later God raised Him bodily from the dead. He then appeared to His disciples, which radically transformed their lives and launched them on a mission that would turn the Roman Empire upside down and eventually impact the entire world.

conclusion

The paragraphs to follow function not just as a conclusion to this chapter, but really as an attempt to tie off all of the chapters dealing with alternative theories, setting the stage for the final section of this book in which we will investigate why some people still find the Easter message difficult to stomach.

To be sure, the resurrection of Jesus Christ was a miracle unparalleled in the history of the world, the hinge on which all of God's story is meant to swing. But Christ conquering the grave was never meant to be a brief moment of mischievous meddling on God's part into the affairs of men and women after long centuries of self-enamored silence and inactivity. God does not, as C.S. Lewis so aptly put it, shake miracles into history at random; there is always a bigger plan at work. The unusual workings of God have a tendency to cluster around climatic moments in redemption history. The New Testament book of Galatians states that, "But when the time had fully come, God sent His Son, born of a woman, born under law, to redeem those under law, that we might receive the full rights of sons." (Galatians 4:4-6)

When Jesus arrived on the scene of human history the Roman 'peace' dominated, one predominant language was spoken across the empire, travel was relatively safe, infrastructure was superb by ancient standards, and the Greek 'gods' had lost much of their oppressive grip on the imaginations of the people. After the long spiritual preparation of humanity, on the edge of an exponential growth in human population, when the time had fully come, God sent His Son to live, die and rise.

Strictly speaking, the resurrection as an isolated historical event doesn't prove anything by itself, other than the world is a stranger place than we once thought. The meaning of the resurrection is determined by the context in which it occurred. When you combine the resurrection with the story of Israel described in the Old Testament, climaxing in the person and work of Jesus; when you add to the mix Jesus' self-understanding, His teachings, His miracles, and His claim to be the one through whom God is restoring all things; then the resurrection becomes a validation of all this and more; almost like God pressed His signet ring into the wax of Jesus' worldview, lifting it out of the realm of religious guesswork and speculation, infusing it with a divine stamp of approval.

More than God's affirming nod in the direction of the veiled-in-flesh deity of Christ, the resurrection becomes a promise, a pledge to our hearts that the world we long for devoid of death, sorrow and unjust suffering is just over the horizon of history.

Just as God launched His first great act of new creation[57] through the resurrection, God's reclamation project will extend to the entirety of this sin-stained world, which will, in due time, be raised up, refurbished, and made shiny and new.[58]

The Easter message was never 'good advice'; we have Dr. Phil for that. Rather, Christianity has always been about good news that provides radical hope in a hurting world. Hope that, in the end, love will win and death will lose; hope that, as Jesus rose, we will rise with Him; hope that the beginning of our story, however bleak and broken, won't determine the end; and hope beyond precious hope that God is with us in Jesus, and one day, we will be with Him, through Jesus.

The Bible tells us that the consequence of our sin is death,[59] not because God is unjust or malicious, but because sin separates you and me from the living God and the life that flows only from Him. Jesus never sinned[60] yet Jesus died, and if the penalty for sin is death and Jesus was free from any transgression, then He must have died not for His own iniquity but for ours.[61] Whereas the

---

57   God created the heavens and the earth with humanity as the crowning apex of God's handiwork (Genesis 1 and 2). Sin entered creation, spoiling and corrupting creation (Genesis 3). God through Jesus is launching a great project of redemption and restoration that will lead to all things in heaven and earth being reconciled to God (Colossians 1). This is what I mean by the resurrection being the first act of new creation, which drags God's future (Revelation 21), a world where death is defeated, into our present reality acting, along with the Holy Spirit in our hearts (Ephesians 1), as a promise of what is to come for the believer.

58   Revelation 21:1-5, 1 Corinthians 15

59   Romans 6:23

60   Hebrews 4:15

61   2 Corinthians 5:21

root of our sin is you and me attempting to substitute ourselves for God, the cause of our salvation is Jesus substituting Himself for us, paying the debt of our sin so that we can be reconciled to our maker. Then God the Father raised Jesus from the dead for our justification so that, through faith alone, in the finished work of Christ alone, to the glory of our great God alone, we may enjoy friendship with our Creator, His people, and together overflow with His forever happiness.

That, and that alone, is our Easter hope in a hurting world, the defeat of death through the death and resurrection of Jesus Christ. So with pen raised and heart full join me in crossing off the list the last of the non-miraculous explanations, the hallucination hypothesis, leaving us face to face with the glorious Gospel of grace.

1	Jesus died	Jesus rose bodily from the dead	**Christianity**
2	Jesus died	Jesus didn't rise— apostles deceivers	~~Conspiracy~~
3	Jesus died	Jesus didn't rise— apostles myth-makers	~~Legend~~
4	Jesus didn't die		~~Swoon~~
5	Jesus died	Jesus didn't rise— apostles deceived	~~Hallucinations~~

CHAPTER SEVEN

miracles or magic

This book in many ways crescendos with the close of the last chapter, striking a wondrous note of hope and, as a result, it is tempting to just let the chord ring on in the mind of the reader as they set this book aside and move on to other matters. But, against my better judgment, I feel the need to tell you a little story. I heard about a gentleman whose mother-in-law passed away while taking a tour of the Holy Land. This man had to fly to Jerusalem and visit the morgue on behalf of the family. Upon arrival he was informed by the mortician that he had two options: he could fly the body of his mother-in-law back to America and pay

25,000 dollars in costs, or he could fork out cash for the Holy Land Discount of 500 dollars. He thought over the matter for a moment and then replied to the mortician, "I am going to pay the 25,000 dollars to ship her back to the States." The mortician was shocked. "Sir, why would you pay that exorbitant fee when she could be buried here for 500?"

Without much pause he responded, "Well, I heard a story about a guy who died and was buried here but three days later he rose from the dead…and I'm not taking any chances with her!"[62]

recapping the resurrection

Look, I don't know why I penned this joke. Is it even funny, or is it just in poor taste?[63] Maybe I was just feeling insecure and hoping that a giggle, or a guffaw, would cause you to be more kindly disposed towards me. Whatever the reason for the brief moment of levity, at this point in our investigation it is appropriate to recap some of the historical data we have explored in the course of our journey together. In chapter three I introduced you to the idea of minimal facts, which represent bedrock historical data that is affirmed by countless scholars across the ideological spectrum. These significant facts must be explained by any historical hypothesis that is proposed. I have suggested that to reasonably deny the bodily resurrection of Jesus, here is what must be plausibly explained in a non-miraculous fashion:

- If the disciples were creating stories about the resur-

---

62   My friend, Jon Morrison, told me this joke.

63   To be clear, I love my mother-in-law.

rection of Jesus, why were women the first witnesses at the empty tomb, considering the fact that their testimony was not considered valid in that culture?

- Why did first century Jewish Christians radically redefine their understanding of the Messiah from a conqueror of the Romans to a suffering servant vindicated by God through the resurrection?

- How did the disciples get away with preaching the resurrection of Jesus in Jerusalem weeks after He was publicly killed there?

- Why did five hundred people at one time claim to see Jesus bodily raised from the dead?

- Why did Jewish men and women, the least likely to confuse God with a human being, come to believe that Jesus was the incarnation of this one true God, right at the beginning of the church?

- How did Paul go from a persecutor of Christians to a fearless missionary?

- How did Jesus' own family, who at one point didn't believe in Him, come to worship Him as Lord, Saviour and God?

The weight of the above evidence has impressed many brilliant and learned individuals. To quote the late Cambridge scholar, Canon Westcott, "Indeed, taking all the evidence together, it is not too much to say that there is no historic incident better or more variously supported than the resurrection of Christ. Nothing but the assumption that it must be false could have suggested a deficiency in the proof of it."[64] Westcott might state his conclusion a little too strongly, but the basic sentiment expressed is exactly right and the direction in which the arguments of this book have been leading us.

We have already succeeded in crossing off the most frequently cited naturalistic explanations for the bedrock historical data surrounding the first Easter event, summarized, in part, above. But, regardless of my attempts to wax eloquent at the closing of the last chapter, I am keenly aware that the conclusion of my argument may be startling for some of my readers, especially if you have surprised yourself by agreeing with the inadequacy of the other proposals that have been commonly offered. Nevertheless, after reaching this point in our investigation, an individual could always shrug their shoulders and say,

"Well, I don't know what happened, but I know the Christian explanation couldn't happen!"

Or,

"I can't explain the above data apart from the resurrection, but I'm sure someone else could. I'm going to hold out for a different answer!"

Or, again,

---

64   As quoted in Paul Little, *Know What You Believe* (Downers Grove, Ill: Intervarsity Press, reprint 2008), 58.

"Those naturalistic explanations may be unlikely but certainly they are more probable than an actual resurrection from the dead!"

All these thoughts and more may be rushing through your mind and, if not, my hunch is that this is exactly how many people will respond to the evidence presented in these pages. For the rest of this chapter we will explore several possible answers to these types of objections that need not be memorized or repeated verbatim but, rather, point the believer in a beneficial direction that may be fruitful when helping people journey through such lingering doubts.

how do you know?

The famous atheist, Bertrand Russell, once said, "In all affairs it's a healthy thing now and then to hang a question mark on the things you have long taken for granted." Let's take Russell's advice for a moment and ask the question, 'How do you or I know that the resurrection couldn't happen?' Is it because resurrections don't normally happen? Is it because we know so much more about our world than the first disciples did? It is certainly true that, thanks to medical science, we know a lot more about dead people *and* living people than the first disciples did. But, here is the key point I want to stress: our increased knowledge has no bearing on the question we are considering in these pages. In fact, the relevant information remains exactly the same for us and the first disciples: dead people normally stay dead, making them insufferably dull participants in a game of hide and seek in this century or any other one.

People in our culture have a tendency to wonder, hasn't modern science advanced in such a way that the miracles in the New Testament are no longer believable? But I think that a moment's honest reflection will expose the superficiality of that popular, but drastically overblown sentiment. After all, in order for this 'pseudo-objection' to be correct, one would have to believe that the first Christians, or the people of the ancient world, did not realize that water was not to be walked on, or that virgins don't actually get pregnant without the involvement of a man, or that water does not, on its own accord, instantaneously transfigure into good wine. All of which are, of course, ridiculous assumptions! No one needed modern science to tell us such things, just common human experience. To quote N.T. Wright:

> A modern myth circulating at the moment says that it's only we who have contemporary post-Enlightenment science who have discovered that dead people don't rise. Those people back then, poor things, were unenlightened, so they believed in all these crazy miracles. But that is simply false...People in the ancient world were incredulous when faced with the Christian claim, because they knew perfectly well that when people die they stay dead.[65]

Most of us are not trained philosophers, but here is what we should realize about miracles. Presupposed in N.T. Wright's comment is the reasonable belief that all miracles actually *assume* a regular and reliable pattern to nature that allows the scientific method to work, and apart from which we would never even be able to

---

65   Antony Flew, *There is a God* (New York, NY: HarperCollins Publisher, 2007), 198.

correctly identify a miracle. Walking on the water is not a recognizable miracle unless people normally sink. In other words, a miracle is an exception. You can't recognize the exception unless you are aware of the general rule that is being broken. When it comes to the resurrection, the general rule that is being broken is the universal nature of death; in this one exceptional moment in time, death is being forced by the author of life to relinquish its grip.

The first disciples knew all this and so do we. In fact, without medical science and our technological advancements, the first disciples knew *better* than we do that dead people have a tendency to stay dead. This generally acknowledged fact is actually a significant part of the Christian case *for* the incredible uniqueness of Jesus, not an objection to it! Because people generally stay dead, Jesus rising from the grave was such a big deal for them and for us! Jesus did things unique in the history of the world because Jesus is actually unique in the history of the world, and never is this more apparent than in His stubborn refusal to stay buried. But, to repeat, it has never been our advanced scientific worldview that has made belief in miracles like the resurrection impossible for us; such a statement is a simply a confusion of thought. Not surprisingly, C.S. Lewis, might state it best:

> If the miracles were offered us as events that normally occurred, then the progress of science, whose business is to tell us what normally occurs, would render belief in them gradually hard and finally impossible. The progress of science has in just this way…made all sorts of things incredible which our ancestors believed;

man-eating ants and gryphons in Scythia, men with one single gigantic foot, magnetic islands that draw all ships towards them, mermaids and fire-breathing dragons. But those things were never put forward as supernatural interruptions of the course of nature. They were put forward as items within her ordinary course…Later and better science has therefore rightly removed them. Miracles are in a wholly different position.…When a thing professes from the very outset to be a unique invasion of nature by something outside, increasing knowledge of nature can never make it either more or less credible than it was at the beginning. In this sense it is mere confusion of thought to suppose that advancing science has made it harder for us to accept miracles.[66]

The scientific method, properly understood and applied, is no real objection to belief in miracles like the resurrection. So what is the problem? Well, I am not entirely sure, but I do think that when one is confronted with the dismal failure of all the non-miraculous explanations of the bedrock historical data, yet still finds themselves unable to believe, it may be helpful to consider three different, but interdependent, matters: the philosophical matter, the historical problem and the personal issue. Investigating each of these categories in turn will allow us to delve more deeply into why some people, when confronted with the evidence for the

---

66   C.S. Lewis, Miracles (New York, NY: HarperCollins Publishers, 1960), 76.

resurrection, still refuse to believe.

philosophical

When considering the resurrection of Jesus Christ, the philosophical issue is: Are miracles possible? Which in turn brings us face to face with the 'God' question. At the beginning of C.S. Lewis's justly famous book, *Miracles*, he has this to say:

> In all my life I have met only one person who claims to have seen a ghost. And the interesting thing about the story is that that person disbelieved in the immortal soul before she saw the ghost and still disbelieves after seeing it. She says that what she saw must have been an illusion or a trick of the nerves. And obviously she may be right. Seeing is not believing. For this reason, the question whether miracles occur can never be answered simply by experience. Every event which might claim a miracle is, in the last resort, something presented to our senses, something seen, heard, touched, smelled, or tasted. And our senses are not infallible. If anything extraordinary seems to have happened, we can always say that we have been the victims of an illusion. **If we hold a philosophy which excludes the supernatural, this is what we always shall say. What we learn from experience depends on the kind of philosophy we bring to experience.**[67]

---

67   C.S. Lewis, *Miracles* (New York, NY: HarperCollins Publishers, 1960), 1-2.

Forgive me for the lengthy quote, but there is so much gold in it that I felt compelled to share it at length. Lewis's point above is bulletproof; if we don't believe in God then miracles are, by definition, impossible. And if we stubbornly refuse to admit the supernatural we will always hold on to even the remotest possibility of a natural explanation, regardless of how unlikely it is, as is so well demonstrated in the quote above. That is why we must settle in our hearts the question of God's existence because, if God exists, then miracles are certainly possible. To quote another Christian philosopher, Norman Geisler:

> If the world had a beginning, then God brought it into existence out of nothing – which is the biggest miracle possible. Thus, if a theistic God exists, not only are miracles possible, but the biggest miracle of all – making something from nothing – has already occurred. Making wine from water (as Jesus did in John 2) is no problem for a God who can make water from nothing![68]

The chart below is intended to help the reader think through the above matter by comparing potential evidence for God creating the universe with the resurrection of Jesus because, as evidenced in Geisler's quote, if you can believe the first verse of the Bible, "In the beginning God created the heavens and the earth"

---

68   Norman L. Geisler, *Twelve Points That Show Christianity is True: A Hand Book on Defending the Christian Faith.* Kindle edition, 2013.

(Genesis 1:1), then you can believe all the other miracles in the rest of the Bible. After all, the God who created nature can certainly invade nature, if He so desires. The chart should be read from left to right:

THE BEGINNING OF THE UNIVERSE	THE RESURRECTION OF JESUS
Unrepeatable, one-time event starting history (kicking off Creation).	Unrepeatable, one-time event in history (kicking off New Creation).
We have never witnessed anything like it.	We have never witnessed anything like it.
There is good evidence for God's existence based on the beginning of the universe, the fine-tuning of the universe, the intelligibility of the universe and our moral and spiritual experience within the universe.	If there is a God, a miracle like a resurrection is possible.

God as an explanation for the existence of the universe, the fine-tuning of the universe, the intelligibility of the universe, and our moral and spiritual experience within the universe, represents a far simpler, far superior explanation than other naturalistic rivals. *This is a big claim that I, sadly, can't defend in this book. But see footnote for recommended resources.[70]	The resurrection as an explanation of the empty tomb, the appearances of Jesus, the transformed lives of His first followers, and the birth of the Christian church, represents a far superior explanation than other naturalistic rivals in simplicity, explanatory scope and explanatory power.

69   William Lane Craig, Reasonable Faith: Christian Truth and Apologetics (Wheaton, Ill: Crossway Books, 1984); William Lane Craig, On Guard: Defending Your Faith with Reason and Precision (Colorado Springs, CO: David C. Cook, 2010); Richard Swinburne, The Existence of God (Oxford, UK: Clarendon Press, 2004); Robert J. Spitzer, New Proofs for the Existence of God: Contributions of Contemporary Physics and Philosophy (Grand Rapids, MI: William B. Eerdmans Publishing, 2010); Timothy Keller, The Reason for God: Belief in an Age of Skepticism (New York NY: Riverhead books, 2008); C.S. Lewis, Mere Christianity (New York, NY: HarperCollins Publishers, reprint 1980).

If there is a God, He created all things out of nothing, which is a greater miracle than a resurrection. So, if you do believe in God, based on the evidence provided by the universe (or an esoteric hunch), you already believe in a greater miracle than the resurrection!	Given Jesus' self-claims and ministry of healing and exorcism, something dramatic occurring after His death is not improbable. When one considers Jesus' own predictions regarding His death and resurrection it should have been anticipated by the disciples and should be unsurprising to us who have the whole story

As the above chart indicates, when we believe in the existence of God, for a wide variety of compelling reasons, we admit that miracles may occur.[70] At the risk of beating this point to death, Antony Flew, one of the most prolific atheistic philosophers of the 20th century, converted to a belief in God based on the type of evidence previously cited. And he wrote at the end of his book, *There is a God*, "Is it possible that there has been or can be divine

---

70   Think of it this way: history is not an exact science. It might be argued that science is not even an exact science. History deals with reconstructions of the past, interpretations of interpretations that lead to one proposing what most likely took place; or in other words, what the most probable explanation of the data in question may be. If there were no God, the probability of a miracle, defined as a supernatural agent interrupting the regularities apparent in the created order, would be exactly zero. But, if God exists, then what is the probability of a miracle? Well, who really knows? How could we know, in fact? If God exists, any *a priori* probabilities are not strictly relevant here, instead, what would be relevant are the historically agreed upon facts and the best explanation of those facts. Therefore, if God exists, we will not arbitrarily conclude that a miracle could not be the best explanation for an event.

revelation? As I said, you cannot limit the possibilities of omnipotence except to produce the logically impossible. Everything else is open to omnipotence."[71] Omnipotence is Flew's own minimalistic descriptive term for God and it is clear from the context that the 'everything' Flew is referring to includes the miraculous.

This admission doesn't, however, negate the fact that whenever an unusual or unlikely event takes place, which may at first glance appear to us as miraculous, it is wise to first seek out a natural explanation to avoid sinking into silly superstition or a 'magical' view of God's activity in His world. A concessionary statement like this should be of great relief to the scientist busily at work in the lab who fears God's arbitrary interference with their experiments. To conclude this section by quoting two scholars:

> Since we all agree that events generally happen in accordance with natural laws, it makes sense to prefer naturalistic explanations over supernatural ones, all other things being equal. But this is quite different from assuming at the outset that all events must be explained in naturalistic terms. A more open-minded, scholarly approach would be to hold that, if all available natural explanations become implausible, we should consider explanations that go beyond the known natural laws that describe how the world generally operates.[72]

---

71   Antony Flew, *There is a God* (New York, NY: HarperCollins Publisher, 2007), 213.

72   Gregory A. Boyd & Paul R. Eddy, *Lord or Legend? Wrestling with the Jesus Dilemma* (Eugene, Oregan: WIPF & STOCK, 2007), 23.

The insight provided in this quotation gives us a general rule of thumb when considering whether or not an unusual event should be classified as a genuine miracle. And, when it comes to Jesus' resurrection, the natural explanations fail to explain the relevant data, leaving us with the only message that the church has ever offered the world: God raised Jesus from the dead.

historical

The historical question is: Are miracles actual? Have they occurred in history? Now, some people, at least at a popular level, are very skeptical about whether or not we can know what really happened regarding any historical event. Yet, often these same people will claim to believe that biological life was spontanously generated on earth in some way or another, though we've never seen that occur in an uncontrolled enviroment. Yes, but that is science, we might protest. True. But it is *historical* science. I am not here to say anything for or against biogenesis or evolutionary theory but, if you believe in it, you believe that we can know what happened in natural history which, of course, includes human history. In any case, when it comes to denying history, Norman Geisler points out that,

> If we cannot know history, then skeptics cannot claim that Christianity is untrue. To say that Christianity is untrue, the skeptic must know history. Why? Because every denial implies an affirmation. To say that Jesus didn't rise from the dead (the denial), the skeptic must know what actually did happen to him (the

affirmation).[73]

As Geisler shows above, to mount a historical case *against* the resurrection of Jesus requires that history can be accurately transmitted and understood by us in the present. Unreasonable skepticism aside, the amount of time between a historical event and us, whether fifty years or a thousand years ago, matters less than we might assume, if we have sources that date close to the events in question that have come from reliable writers and that have reached us basically as they were written. If you remember earlier chapters, you will recall that all three of these criteria are met by the Christian Gospels and, in particular, the early Christian creed I introduced in chapter three.

biases

Other readers may be concerned about the biases inherent in all historical writers. To quote N.T. Wright once more, "It must be asserted most strongly that to discover a particular writer has a bias tells us nothing whatever about the value of the information he or she presents. It merely bids us be aware of the bias (and our own, for that matter), and to assess the material according to as many sources as we can."[74] We all have our biases, especially regarding a matter as important as the resurrection of Jesus. But what follows from that admission? Does that mean we can never

---

73   Norman Geisler & Frank Turek, *I Don't Have Enough Faith to be an Atheist*. (Wheaton, Illinois: Crossway books, 2004), 232.

74   N.T. Wright, *The New Testament People of God* (Minneapolis: Fortress Press, 1992), 89.

report anything accurately or tell the truth about events? Of course not! In fact, sometimes the exact opposite is true. For example, Jewish writers wrote the most accurate accounts of the holocaust and, in this case, their scrupulous accuracy was motivated by their biases and their strong desire to let the world know exactly what happened to their people.[75] When considering the first followers of Jesus, one could imagine the disciples carefully preserving the stories about Him *because* they loved Him so much. Not only that, as we have seen in this book, not everyone reported to be eyewitnesses to the resurrection were biased in favour of Jesus. James was a skeptic, and Paul hated Christians. Both were biased against belief; that is, until Jesus appeared to them.

history is unknowable

In other instances, the problem is not that history is ultimately unknowable, though certainty may elude us, but rather that some historians remain reticent to adjudicate on whether or not a miracle occurred when working as a historian. The reasons for this may be a philosophical prejudice or the belief that, when working in historiography to explain bygone events, one must proceed from generally accepted causal factors, without invoking the supernatural.

This practice might not be all bad, but it still seems that an unwillingness to conclude that miracles have happened in history might be overly restrictive and ultimately unwarranted. For

---

75   Scholar Craig Blomberg points this out in *Real Answers: Jesus, the Search Continues* (produced for Inspiration Network), Tape 1. A transcript of this video series is available at *www.insp.com/jesus/transcripts.htm*

example, when considering the topic of this book, because we do possess a multitude of sources for the first Easter event, written closely enough to the event in question and even containing the remembrances of eyewitnesses, we should feel liberated (methodologically speaking) to piece together the events of the first Easter with the normal tools of historical investigation. And once we recognize that God's miraculous activity continues in the present, it might make good sense to consider the miraculous as a live option to explain unusual historical events in the past, especially when natural hypotheses are stretched beyond their breaking points. This statement, of course, raises the question as to whether or not miracles actually occur today.

Craig Keener, an accomplished scholar and the author of a two-volume work entitled, *Miracles*, carefully documents over a thousand pages of present day miracle reports. These reports are culled from all around the globe and contain events that seem to defy any type of naturalistic explanation. In some cases Keener knew the people who witnessed or experienced the apparent miracle themselves, including an incident in his own family. In fact, here is what one skeptic, who happens to be a trained physician, wrote after reading Keener's book:

> I was ready to "see through" yet another theologian who didn't know much about psychosomatic illnesses, temporary improvements with no long-term follow up, incorrect medical diagnoses, conversion disorders, faked cures, self-deception, and the like…So I opened the book, ploughed through the philosophi-

cal chapters, and came to the chapters of case studies. I was blind-sided.

Keener reports literally thousands of cases in these two volumes. I read them with the critical eye of a skeptic having many years of medical practice under the belt. I found many reports to be unreliable. In most other cases where reporting seemed accurate, I could see alternative, naturalistic explanations for the cures.

But "most" cases is not the same thing as "all." Not by a long shot. And it was the minority (still numbering in the hundreds) that I found to be stunning. They couldn't just be dismissed with a knowing answer and a cheery wave of the hand. With respect to my worldview, I had had the chair pulled out from underneath me.[76]

I have read Dr. Keener's book as well. I don't share this critic's negative assessment, in that I am willing to admit that more of the reports are credible than he is, but his admission above is important because it comes from a hardened skeptic who is trained in the medical field.

My frustration is that many people in our day claim that religious people are close-minded, but often it is the street-level skeptic who appears too close-minded to admit even the possibility of a tiny miracle. From our limited experience we cast a net over all of reality, through which no miracle can pass. And, unlike our unbelieving friend quoted above, we do all of this without

---

76   Quote found on Philip Yancey's Site: http://philipyancey.com/jesus-and-miracles

even taking the time to investigate, with an open mind, all the claimed miracles in our world, many of them made by 'enlightened', educated individuals who, prior to witnessing the miracle, didn't believe that God performed them or that God even existed at all. I am hoping that my reader would have a more open mind.

I work part-time for an organization called Alpha that produces videos that help young people have conversations about life, faith and the significance of Jesus. In the Alpha Youth Film Series there is a lesson on the fact that God still heals people miraculously today. Because I believe this to be true, I love that Alpha gives everyone an opportunity to receive prayer for healing and, because I am a part of the Alpha writing process, occasionally I get to hear about amazing stories of healing.

There is a youth group at a church near my home, for example, that was doing the Youth Alpha course. They watched the video on healing and afterwards they prayed for a young girl who had scars on her arms from cutting herself. She often wore long sleeves because she was embarrassed about all the marks she had carved into her skin. But, as her friends prayed for her, they watched in amazement as the scars started to fade and disappear right in front of their eyes. Apparently, a bit of screaming, amazement and celebration ensued.

I could easily multiply stories like this that come from reasonable, reliable, educated individuals, but I love the kindness of God and His willingness to remove these visible sources of shame in this girl's life. This story also reminds me that a physical healing like this one, though amazing, doesn't actually touch our deepest need. How much more important is it to have the brokenness inside of us that would cause us to hurt ourselves in the first place, healed by the love of God and mended by the mercy of our gracious Father.

the problem with miracles

As a pastor I am acutely aware that any discussion about miracles at once creates a problem. Why does God intervene surprisingly and obviously in some situations and not others? I don't pretend to know the answer to this predicament. I am sure that the seemingly discriminate nature of miracles was also a problem for witnesses of Jesus' own ministry when some were healed and some were not. Despite my ignorance regarding this matter, I take great hope in the fact that Jesus' miracles and, ultimately, His resurrection, are signposts directing us to the character of God and the nature of His kingdom.

As mentioned in the last chapter, Jesus' powerful acts were signs of a future reality breaking into our present pain, promises of a world filled with healing and wholeness that will one day arrive when God restores all things. Jesus gives us a taste of God's promised future to whet our lips in anticipation of what is to come and to keep us thirsting for the appearing of His kingdom in its fullness. Until that day, healing miracles in this life are partial and we will all eventually die of something.

To reiterate the overarching point of this section, however, the inscrutable nature of God's seemingly discriminate sprinkling of miracles into history doesn't negate the truth that God still works in surprising ways in our day, lending strong support to the Biblical worldview that permits a supernatural act like the resurrection. But, in the end, whether we are ever willing to accept a miracle or not will lead us to the personal question.

personal

David Hume, the notorious 18th century skeptic, once wrote, "Upon the whole, we may conclude, that the Christian religion not only was first attended with miracles, but even at this day cannot be believed by any reasonable person without one."[77] These are clever but mocking words. Hume claims that, for a smart person to believe the Christian faith would require a miracle. And, for once I actually agree with David Hume. One definition of a miracle would be the invasion of a supernatural entity into the natural realm, and, if this were a defensible definition, what Hume says would be true. To truly believe in Christ requires a miracle. God must raise our hearts from the dead.

In his letter to the Ephesians, the Apostle Paul writes that,

> As for you, you were dead in your transgressions and sins, in which you used to live when you followed the ways of this world and of the ruler of the kingdom of the air, the spirit who is now at work in the sons of disobedience…Like the rest, we were by nature objects of wrath. But because of His great love for us, God, who is rich in mercy, made us alive with Christ even when we were dead in transgressions – it is by grace you have been

---

77   *Essay on Miracles part 2* David Hume, Dialogues Concerning Natural Religion 125It

saved. (Eph. 2:1-5)

We were all dead in our sins, unresponsive to God, hearts dull, heads dim, unbelieving wills mired in sin. The picture is a bleak one without the intervening grace of a merciful, beautiful, loving God who willingly reaches into our lives and removes the veil of unbelief. Breathing life into a dead heart is a miracle of grace; an unearned, ill-deserved miracle that takes place in the lives of all believers through the work of the Holy Spirit. God does this miracle because God loves us. God's love that is so vast, deep and breathtakingly expansive, His affection that is as broad as the heavens and as close as the secret cracks in our hearts, reaches down into the muck and mire of our lives to love us into liberation through His Son, Jesus.

This is our radical hope in a hurting world.

Miracles of grace aside, the personal question is the crux of the issue: If an individual doesn't believe in God, they will resist the conclusion of this extended argument, if an individual believes in God, but doesn't want to follow Jesus, they will resist the reality of the resurrection in their heart and in history. Both of these responses tell an individual a lot about their psyche and worldview commitments, but it still doesn't discount the fact that the resurrection is the best explanation of the historical data explored in this book.

conclusion

To be honest, I believe that an even stronger historical case for the resurrection could be made, but a more robust argument would require many more pages and that might stretch your interest and attentiveness beyond the breaking point. I know some of you have been keenly tested already. As a result, this short book has failed to provide the reader with other significant historical evidence for the resurrection including: the first disciples imparting saving significance to Jesus' death, a theological move that would be nonsensical and absurd apart from the resurrection occurring; or their surprising reworking of the standard Jewish messianic expectations that looked for a political military leader overthrowing the Romans, not a suffering servant, dying on a cross and being vindicated by a resurrection. Space doesn't permit us to discuss the first disciples changing their day of worship from Saturday to Sunday, overthrowing centuries of religious observance; or the radical mutation that took place in their beliefs about the Jewish law in light of Jesus.

On and on we could go. And if one thinks the above mutations that occurred in the distinctly Jewish worldview of Jesus' first followers are insignificant or humdrum that just shows (forgive me for saying it) profound ignorance about the religious life of Jewish people in first century Palestine and their fierce commitment to their religious tradition; traditions that held together their unique cultural identity in the midst of hostile nations for century after century. To make these significant changes in their theology and their understanding of the nature of God, apart from the resurrection actually occurring, is very difficult to understand. So to conclude this brief exploration of the personal, historical and philosophical issues surrounding the resurrection, I will call to the stand the testimony of two expert witnesses. Cambridge historian, C.F.D. Moule concludes:

> The birth and rapid rise of the Christian church…
> remain an unsolved enigma for any historian who re-
> fuses to take seriously the only explanation offered by
> the church itself.[78]

N.T. Wright, who wrote a 700-page book on the resurrection, claims:

> The easiest explanation by far is that these things hap-
> pened because Jesus really was raised from the dead,
> and the disciples really did meet Him, even though
> His body was renewed and transformed…The resur-
> rection of Jesus does in fact provide a sufficient expla-
> nation for the empty tomb and the meetings with Je-
> sus. Having examined all the possible hypotheses I've
> read about anywhere in literature, I think it is also a
> necessary explanation.[79]

The learned evaluation of these men, though interesting, won't matter much in the end, at least for you or for I. All of the scholarly words quoted throughout the course of this work won't count a whit in the last moments of our lives. The only question that will be of ultimate importance is: What do you, the reader, say?

---

78   C.F.D. Moule, *The Phenomenon of the New Testament* (London: SCM Press, 1967), 13.

79   Antony Flew, *There is a God* (New York, NY: HarperCollins Publisher, 2007), 212.

So imagine Jesus asking you the question He asked His disciples so many years ago, "Who do you say that I am?"[80] What would your answer be?

I hope and pray it would echo the words of the iconic doubter, Thomas. 'My Lord and my God.'

Because, "If you declare with your mouth, 'Jesus is Lord,' and believe in your heart that God raised Him from the dead, you will be saved." (Romans 10:9)

And I hope and pray this book helped, by God's grace, to get you there.

---

80   Mark 8:29

[HAPTER EIGHT

radical hope in a hurting world

I was in church when I heard the news. A high-school friend had been paddling late one night through the frigid waters of a Whistler Lake. His canoe flipped and he was, shortly thereafter, reported to us as missing. When I was informed of the crisis I forgot to pray. Instead it felt like I held my breath until a search party found his body the next day. I exhaled with a curse hurled at the heavens.

A rush of memories can flood your mind in the midst of loss; countless tales of laughter, stupidity, kindness and conversation. It can be overwhelming, raw and all-consuming for a time, like an orifice has been pried open in the placid surface of your life and into the crack rushes a flood of violent emotions you don't feel like feeling. And there I was, in church, newly awakened to faith, months old in the Lord; freshly initiated into the eternal mysteries, the translucent nature of heaven and the opaque nature of hell, mourning the loss of a friend. My faith didn't take away the ache, either because my faith was too new or my loss was too present or, perhaps for some other reason all together. The lump in my throat didn't lessen. The pain in my chest didn't disappear. I grieved as grievers do.

Death was still an enemy.

The difference for me, I guess, was that now death was an enemy living in a world where God raised His Son from the dead which, of course, is the type of difference that makes all the difference in the long run. In the short run, to be sure, this is still a world where the only thing that will stop us from watching everyone we love die of disease, accident or crime, is our own death from disease, accident or crime. But the world was this way before I was given belief.

Suffering was a stubborn part of my pre-conversion data. I had been to funerals before and I had spent some morbid moments reflecting on the inevitability of my own. Only a fateful step away, I had been told. I knew, at least from a distance, the tragic/comic nature of human life on this pale, blue dot floating through the darkness. I knew the mortality rate was 100 percent. Or, I should say, I knew all this in my head; there is room to doubt whether or not I knew all this in my heart. Sadly, sometimes our heart has to be hit hard before it truly awakens to the rough edges of reality and learns to really feel the weight of tragedy.

Yet, there was a difference that faith made in my mourning; a change, not in the world, but a change in me. The shift was, and still is, that I've had my ear tuned to the whispered rumours of another world, a world whose waves of love, hope and redemption have started to crash unceasingly on the shores of this tired, old, ill-behaved planet.

We suck oxygen in a world where God raised His Son from the dead and, in that, there is hope for wholeness.

Hope that those beautiful stories, so filled with struggle, hardship, death and sacrifice, yet ending with a happiness made brighter, not by the absence of scars, but by their unfortunate acquisition, are not just the stuff of fairy tales and bedside stories that haunt our memories before our hearts filled up with hurt. Rather, fairy tales are the echoes of this, this real story, filled with quirky, hard-done-by characters, sinners longing to be saints and saints confessing they are sinners. This story that stoops to sweep up and include people like you and me, straining at the oars of life, leaning into the wind, heading for God's celestial shore, hopefully with the needed help of His hand. Eyes blinkered and weighed down with hot tears that can obscure, but never quite sweep away the sight of a blood-stained cross and an empty tomb that whisper, steadily and persistently, 'I love you still; all is not lost. If God is for you, who, my friend, can be against you? Your heart beats in a world where God raised His Son from the dead. The world hasn't stopped spinning and God hasn't stopped saving. In that there truly is a hope that is stronger than death.

love wins

In an atheistic universe, death ultimately wins and love ultimately loses. Count the cost. Deny God, then deny yourself and all the significance or your loves and losses, and follow me into oblivion. Gain the world and lose your soul, then lose the world too. The story ends here. It all started with a bang, but it won't even implode with a whimper; a whimper is too dignified a response in the face of the oncoming darkness.

A godless universe keeps death and suffering while removing meaningful freedom and God; it also creates and sustains the problem of ultimate hopelessness; all of that without even a deity to complain to about (or blame for) our sorry situation. There is only what '*is*', not what '*ought*' to be; the dignity of coherent revolt is replaced by a tired resignation in light of injustice, hardship and innumerable sufferings. You see, anger *implies* an 'ought.' Justice *requires* an 'ought.' Atheism can only provide an 'is.' The universe *is* what it is. Did you expect it to be something else? Terrible, I know. I am almost sorry to disappoint you.

Only God provides the 'ought' that calls what *is* to account, the transcendent standard of good that cultural conventions must bow before, acts of kindness must conform to, and acts of cruelty must flee from. There is a way the world ought to be and somewhere, deep down, you know this to be true. After all, you've protested, you've voted; you've found nature to be strangely unnatural. You are still a stranger at home because you were made for God's New Heavens and New Earth.

And this, thankfully, is not it.

One day, some day, this world will be made ready and the

crooked lines we've drawn will be straightened out by the ultimate author; in this way what '*is*' will reflect what '*ought*' to be; the distance will be bridged, the unlawful divorce will be reconciled; heaven will invade earth, not incognito, but fully and finally.

You belong to this future world, Christian; you are citizens of heaven manning outposts on earth, pockets of light pushing back the darkness and testifying to the coming dawn. Dress yourself in loving kindness then, clothe yourself in Christ; all in eager anticipation of that moment when the tyranny of what 'is' will be tossed into the dustbin of history.

In the Christian story love wins and death loses. The resurrection turns death from a period or a question mark into a comma, after which follows the climax and continuation of God's story into a New Heavens and New Earth. Death remains an enemy for us, but a defeated enemy, which, in the hands of a redemptive God, can now be employed by Him as the great healer. Instead of disease ending solely in our demise, death for us becomes the end of all disease, hardship and suffering as we enter, through loving trust in the blood of Jesus, into God's future world; bearing the marks of our suffering, perhaps, but marks that, on our new resurrection bodies, only increase our glory. For, in that moment, we will be like the resurrected Christ in all of His glory. This is our hope. There is a better, more beautiful story to live in than the barren, hope-sucking quagmire of atheism.

So, the only question is, which story do you want to live in through all your loves and losses? Which tale do you want your life to tell?

The choice is yours.

For me, the words of the apostle Paul at the end of his treatise on the resurrection seem a fitting conclusion:

> Therefore, my dear brothers and sisters, stand firm. Let nothing move you. Always give yourselves fully to the work of the Lord, because you know that your labour in the Lord is not in vain. (1 Corinthians 15:58)

APPENDIX ONE

the pagan christ

Several years ago the mockumentary *Religulous* attempted to show that the account of Jesus was borrowed from pagan mystery religions that flourished throughout the Roman Empire. This is a tired, dated argument, but it remains popular in certain circles. In this short appendix I want to discuss three 'rules' for assessing the accusation that the first Christians were plagiarizing the pagans. (I use the word 'pagan' throughout this appendix as a descriptive, rather than a derisive term.)[81]

---

81   For a more thorough examination of these arguments see Mary Jo Sharp's essay entitled, "Does the Story of Jesus Mimic Pagan Mystery Stories?" found in the book, *Come Let Us Reason Together*. Also, see the essay "Challenging the Zeitgeist Movie" by Mark W. Foreman found in the aforementioned volume.

rule one: check the sources

Despite the popular but exaggerated claims on the world-wide web, historians have long since refuted the sensational claim that the resurrection of Jesus, to give one highly significant example, was 'stolen' from pagan myths like the story of Osiris, Isis and Horus. Thankfully, one can read many of these ancient myths by searching the Internet (and primary sources are always best!). In the case of Osiris and Isis, a cursory reading of this Egyptian tale[82] will prove to any objective reader that there are no relevant similarities between the resurrection of Christ and this Egyptian story, whether in teaching or literary genre. Osiris wasn't resurrected in the Jewish or Christian sense of the word, he undergoes a crude resuscitation but only to live on in the underworld, his shredded body pieced together by his devoted wife, Isis.

From this example we learn that the **first rule** when encountering the assertion that the first Christians copied pagan mystery religions is, when possible, to read the pagan stories yourself (in original sources like *The Egyptian Book of the Dead*[83]) and then compare them to the Christian Gospels. Often the alleged similarities are just not there.

---

82   There are actually at least two different versions but my comments would apply to both.

83   This advice would be hard to apply in the case of Mithras, which contains no substantive written record. However, this should make one wary about the validity of any alleged parallels between the cult of Mithras and Christianity. For example, Mithras is called the saviour, but our only evidence of this commons from a single inscription that post-dates Christianity. P. 157 of *Come Let Us Reason Together*.

rule 2: check the date

He was a first century itinerant preacher. He gathered follow-ers, performed miracles and convinced others that he was more than human. He was known as the Son of God. He ran afoul of the Roman authorities and was put on trial. His body was killed but His soul could not die and He ascended to heaven where He continues to live. To prove His continued existence after His death He appeared to at least one of His doubting followers. Do you recognize this description? It sounds a lot like Jesus of Naza-reth. But it is not. This is a description of a man named Apollo-nius who lived around the time of Jesus.

Many skeptical scholars make much of the corresponding ca-reers of Jesus and Apollonius. But what is often conveniently left out in the above accounting is that the stories of Apollonius were written down in the third century CE by a man named Philostra-tus. That means that the stories about Apollonius postdate the Gospels by several hundred years. If Philostratus was writing long after the Gospel authors while Christianity was rapidly spreading throughout the Roman Empire, who do you think was copying from whom? The answer should be obvious.

The **second rule** when encountering these sensational copy-cat claims is to research when the alleged similarities appear in the pagan texts. The mystery religions were syncretistic, and if the parallels post-date the Christian Gospels you can be assured that, if there was borrowing, the pagans were most likely the ones guilty of it.[84]

rule 3: expect some real similarities

The points of contact that do exist between the pagan myths and Christianity represent commonalities that are prevalent in most religions. Examples would include salvation motifs/promises of immortality and the use of light and darkness as metaphors; and it is fallacious to suppose that this type of correlation necessarily implies causation. C.S. Lewis taught us how to think about these possible points of congruence years ago in a remarkable essay entitled, *Is Theology Poetry?*

> What light is really thrown on the truth or falsehood of Christian Theology by the occurrence of similar ideas in Pagan religion? Supposing for purposes of argument, that Christianity is true; then it could avoid all coincidence with other religions only on the supposition that all other religions are one hundred percent erroneous…The Truth is that the resemblances tell nothing for or against the truth of Christian theology. If you start from the assumption that the Theology is false, the resemblances are quite consistent with that assumption… But if you start with the as-

---

84   The two examples chosen above, involving the Egyptian tale of Horus and Isis and the stories about Apollonius, are noteworthy because they are typical of other alleged comparisons between Christianity and the pagan mystery religions (i.e. the cults of Dionysus or Mithras); the similarities are non-existent, exaggerated, and/or post–date the growth and spread of Christianity (e.g. stories about Apollonius).

sumption that the Theology is true, the resemblances fit equally well. Theology, while saying that a special illumination has been vouchsafed to Christians and (earlier) to Jews, also says that there is some divine illumination vouchsafed to all men…We should, therefore, expect to find in the imagination of great Pagan teachers and myth makers some glimpse of that theme which we believe to be the very plot of the whole cosmic story – the theme of incarnation, death, and rebirth.[85]

The **third rule** is that some of these parallels should be expected. The difference between Christianity and the pagan myths, Lewis goes on to point out, is that the Gospels are historical writings that intend to record the facts of what really happened to Jesus of Nazareth and, therefore, don't bear the literary characteristics of myths.

conclusion

In conclusion, it is worth noting that there is no historical data that the mystery religions were prevalent in first century Palestine. Moreover, there is significant historical data that indicates first century Jews were fiercely resistant to pagan ideas (especially when marched into town in the oppressive boots of the Roman army, e.g. The Cult of Mithras), making it unthinkable that the

---

85   C.S. Lewis, "Is Theology Poetry?" *The Weight of Glory* (New York, NY: Harper-Collins Publishers, 2001), 127,128.

first Jewish disciples of Jesus would construct stories about His ministry or His resurrection based on these pagan mythologies. These provocative but ill-founded assertions represent a school of comparative religion that was, at one time, prevalent in Germany, but is now close to a hundred years out of date. Responsible scholarship has moved on and so should we.[86]

---

86   For the best refutation of this idea see Ronald H. Nash, *The Gospel and the Greeks: Did the New Testament Borrow from Pagan Thought?* (New Jersey, NY: P & R Publishing, 1992).

BIBLIOGRAPHY

Antony Flew, *There is a God* (New York, NY: HarperCollins Publisher, 2007)

Bart D. Ehrman, *Forged: Writing in the Name of God – Why the Bible's Authors are not who we think they are* (New York, NY: HarperCollins Publishers, 2011)

C.S. Lewis, *The Problem of Pain* (New York, NY: HarperCollins Publishers, 1940)

C.S. Lewis, *Miracles* (New York, NY: HarperCollins Publishers, 1960)

C.S. Lewis, "Modern Theology and Biblical Criticism." In, *The Collected Works of C.S. Lewis* (New York, NY: Inspirational Press, 1996)

C.S. Lewis, "Is Theology Poetry?" *The Weight of Glory* (New York, NY: HarperCollins Publishers, 2001)

David Hume, *Dialogues Concerning Natural Religion,* "Essay on Miracles part 2."

David Bagget, ed., *Did the Resurrection Happen? A Conversation with Gary Habermas and Antony Flew* (Downers Grove, Ill: Intervarsity Press, 2009)

E.P. Sanders, *The Historical Figure of Jesus* (New York: NY, Penguin Books, 1983)

F.F. Bruce, *The New Testament Documents: Are they reliable?* (Downers Grove, Ill: Intervarsity Press, 1943)

J.D, Crossan & Jonathan L. Reed. *Excavating Jesus: Beneath the Stones, Behind the Texts.* (New York: NY, HarperSanFrancisco, A Division of HarperCollins Publishers, 2001)

Jim Warner Wallace, *Cold-Case Christianity* (Colorado Springs, CO: David C. Cook, 2013)

John Dominic Crossan, *Jesus: A Revolutionary Biography* (San Francisco: HarperCollings, 1991)

Gerd, Lüdemann. *The Resurrection of Jesus Christ: A Historical Inquiry* (Amherst, NY: Prometheus, 2004)

Gary Habermas & Michael Licona, *The Case for the Resurrection of Jesus* (Grand Rapids, MI: Kregel Publications, 2004)

Gregory A. Boyd & Paul R. Eddy, *Lord or Legend? Wrestling with the Jesus Dilemma* (Eugene, Oregan: WIPF & STOCK, 2007)

Josh McDowell & Dave Sterrett, *Did the Resurrection happen… Really?* (Chicago, Ill: Moody Publishers, 2011)

Mark Driscoll & Gerry Breshears, *Doctrine: What Christians Should Believe (*Wheaton, Ill: Crossway Publishing, 2010*)*

Norman Geisler & Frank Turek, *I Don't have enough Faith to be an Atheist.* (Wheaton, Illinois: Crossway books, 2004)

Norman L. Geisler, *Twelve Points That Show Christianity is True: A Hand Book on Defending the Christian Faith.* (Kindle edition, 2013)

Paul Copan, ed., *Will the Real Jesus Please Stand Up? A Debate between William Lane Craig and John Dominic Crossan* (Grand Rapids, MI: Baker Publishing, 1998)

Paul Little, *Know What You Believe* (Downers Grove, Ill: Intervarsity Press, reprint 2008)

Peter Kreeft & Ronald K. Tacelli, *Handbook of Christian Apologetics* (Downers Grove, Ill: Intervarsity press, 1994)

Paul, Barnett, *Is the New Testament Reliable?* (Downers Grover, Ill: Intervarsity Press, 2003)

N.T. Wright, *The New Testament People of God* (Minneapolis: Fortress Press, 1992)

N.T. Wright, *The Resurrection of the Son of God* (Minneapolis: Fortress Press, 2003)

Ronald H. Nash, *The Gospel and the Greeks: Did the New Testament Borrow from Pagan Thought?* (New Jersey, NY: P & R Publishing, 1992)

William Lane Craig, *The Son Rises: The Historical Evidence for the Resurrection of Jesus* (Eugene, Oregon: Wipf and Stock Publishers, 1981)

about the author

Chris Price is the lead pastor at Calvary Baptist Church (*www. calvarybaptist.ca*) and the author of *Suffering with God*, published by Apologetics Canada (*www.apologeticscanada.com*). He lives in Port Coquitlam, B.C. with his beautiful wife Diandra and his two children Kaeden and Mila. You can follow him on twitter @topherjprice or email him at topherprice@hotmail.com

53004930R00075

Made in the USA
Charleston, SC
03 March 2016